THE
DMS HANDBOOK

James Adlam
Keith Hamer

Capital Transport

INTRODUCTION

London Transport's DMS had a complicated history of ups and downs. Even before delivery was completed, LT had marked the type down for an early withdrawal, yet the economic climate of the 1980s allowed the DMS to bounce back into favour, managing some twenty years of service in London. Meanwhile, operators around Britain (and beyond) discovered the DMS, many of them being rewarded by years of successful service. This book looks at the history of the DMS and its derivatives both in London and elsewhere.

Thanks are due to the many subsequent owners who have assisted in the task of obtaining photographs of DMSs in new colours and uses, and also to the PSV Circle and Lawrie Bowles for information.

ISBN 185414 171 6

Published by Capital Transport Publishing
38 Long Elmes, Harrow Weald, Middlesex

Printed by Bath Midway Press,
Midlands Industrial Estate, Holt, Wiltshire

CONTENTS

Front cover Former DMS 620 has spent most of its life in London, operating when first sold on the Culturebus sightseeing service. It then spent a short time in Southend before returning to the Ensignbus fleet. It is now with the Lambeth Community Youth Steel Orchestra and is seen outside St Pauls Cathedral during a lunchtime concert in August 1994. *N J Eadon-Clarke*

Frontispiece Former DMS 1469 has had a very varied career. It operated on various London sight-seeing tours before joining the Ensignbus fleet. During 1987 it was converted into an exhibition unit by the Ensign workshops for The Department of Employment and toured the country in 1988. It is seen in Kidbrooke, south London in August of that year. *N J Eadon-Clarke*

Back cover upper DMT 2413 is now a dedicated trainer with London General, hence the panelled over blind box, special livery and re-classification to DMT. It is seen at the North Weald Rally in 1993 on the 'Drive a Bus' circuit. *N J Eadon-Clarke*

Back cover lower Three examples in the fleet of Bryans of Enfield; former DM 1070 stands next to DMS 1890 and Iveco engined DMS 2411. These vehicles are regular performers on contract work in the Capital and were photographed in August 1994. *N J Eadon-Clarke*

Two DMSs were displayed at the 1970 Commercial Motor Show at Earls Court, DMS 1 on the Park Royal Vehicles stand and DMS 2 on Daimler's stand. DMS 1 kept its Leyland badge for at least its first year in service; DMS 2 entered service without it.
Colin Brown

Before 1966, bus operators were required by law to have conductors on all double-deckers; this encouraged them to turn to high-capacity single-deckers. In the late 1960s, London Transport introduced hundreds of driver-only single-deckers and Automatic Fare Collection (AFC) machinery was often used to speed boarding.

London Transport's first rear-engined double-deckers, 50 Leyland Atlanteans (XAs) and eight Daimler Fleetlines (XFs), arrived in 1965, still needing conductors. In 1969 LT converted the 50 XAs for one-person-operation (OPO) and on 22nd November 1969 XA 22 became London's first OPO double-decker on route 233, Roundshaw–West Croydon, soon followed by the other XAs at Peckham and Croydon. Meanwhile, with one-person-operation legalised for double-deckers, LT's designers started work on a new standard bus for the 1970s: a purpose-built high capacity OPO vehicle.

London Transport preferred to design its vehicles from scratch, but British Leyland already had three double-deck chassis on offer and had no wish to produce another purely for LT. Also, the Government's new 'Bus Grant' (up to 25% of the cost of any new bus) was only paid on manufacturers' standard vehicles.

London Transport chose the Daimler Fleetline after good results from the XFs. The Fleetline was more reliable than the Atlantean, and the separately mounted engine and gearbox eased cooling and maintenance. The Fleetline meant a return to body-on-chassis construction, leaf springs and air brakes, all features which had been discarded on the Routemaster. However, the 10.45 litre Gardner 6LXB engine produced 170bhp, making this more powerful than any previous London double-decker; the gearbox was fully automatic. As the engine compartment projected beyond the lower deck rear wall, cosmetic shrouds were designed to fill the gap above.

The body was designed within a length of 30ft 10ins. The entrance and forward gangway was divided; passengers could enter at the very front and pay the driver (who had an Almex ticket machine) or enter by the rear half and use the AFC machine, which issued a range of tickets and released a turnstile. To create circulating space, a single forward-facing seat was fitted between the AFC and the centre exit. Seating was H44/24D, but with room for 21 standing the total capacity was a creditable 89. LT used their own cab design with raised driving position, rounded instrument console, public address systems, and a periscope.

The external body design, initially built by Park Royal Vehicles, was bold and angular and owed a lot to the single deckers, especially the shape of the windscreen. The bold styling was let down by a new drab livery of unrelieved red, with an LT outline bullseye on each side. The shortlived 'coin in the slot' logo was displayed on the front at first.

LT ordered a trial batch of 17 DMSs for 1969 delivery, but there were serious delays at Daimler, partly due to high demand. A second batch of 100 was ordered for 1970 to protect continuity. No DMSs had arrived by mid-1970, but 250 more were ordered for 1971, so that all 367 arrived continuously. The first ones appeared in September 1970 when DMS 1 and DMS 2 were displayed at the Commercial Motor Show. A press launch took place on 31st December 1970 at Victoria garage, using DMS 38, bearing 'The Londoner Bus' posters: LT's marketing of the DMS as the 'Londoner' failed to catch the public's imagination.

Route 4A (Finsbury Park–Waterloo) had been chosen as the trial route for the original group of 17 vehicles, but with 350 more on order there was no point in a trial operation. Full scale introduction of DMSs got under way on 2nd January 1971 on routes 95 (Tooting Broadway–Cannon Street) and 220 (Harlesden–Tooting), from Brixton and Shepherds Bush garages: DMS 1 was first into service on the 220. Initially, passengers accepted the DMS much more willingly than the OPO single-deckers because of the higher seating capacity.

The Cannon Street terminus of route 95 in the first week of DMS operation. The 'coin in the slot' symbols were displayed to alert passengers to the fact that AFC equipment was installed. Few people noticed.
London Transport Museum

**Interior views of
the DMS when new.**
London Transport
Museum

The third route to gain DMSs was Holloway's 271 on 16th January, followed by Merton's 189 on 30th January. On these four routes, DMSs operated with pre-decimal currency, but LT changed over on 21st February 1971. DMS 72 then entered service from Shepherds Bush with an experimental AFC machine made by Setright: it issued tickets from a roll instead of a folded pack as on the previous Bell Punch AFC, which had been giving some problems. The 'coin in the slot' symbol was phased out at about the same time.

September-October 1971 saw the first of the third batch, DMS 118-367. DMS 118-167 had the same body design as before and were coded 2/1DM1, but from DMS 168 the headlamps were moved further apart, improving the appearance and making the bus more visible at night: 168-367 were coded 2/1DM1/2.

Realising how plain the all-red livery looked, LT put a white waist band down each side of DMS 76, and this livery was adopted for DMSs 118-367. The rarely-used external public address was now omitted. LT had decided to change to Setright AFCs, and these were fitted to DMSs 158-284 and 368 onwards. All Bell Punch units had been replaced by the end of 1972.

Although the Gardner engine was Daimler's standard, a Leyland 0680 was also offered and LT decided to try it. DMS 132 was experimentally fitted with an 0680 and entered service in July 1971, classified 1/2DM1.

The plain all-red livery applied to DMSs was felt to be in need of some relief. After a trial application of a white band each side on DMS 76, a batch of DMSs from DMS 118 was also given these. Whether it improved the appearance of the buses is arguable, but the livery modification lasted only up to the delivery of DMS 367. John Fozard

Yellow doors were originally introduced on DMSs (and also SMSs) to indicate a bus with AFC equipment. Coincident with this was the change from an outline bullseye logo to a solid white roundel below the front upper deck side windows. Capital Transport

Early routes converted to DMS suffered a reduction in vehicle allocation and frequency. LT felt this was justified by the DMS's capacity of 89 people, compared with 61-77 on crew buses, but the slower boarding times compared with the crew buses they replaced meant that this economy could not be sustained. From 30th October 1971, when Bexleyheath's 96 was converted, each crew bus was replaced by one DMS, which made the exercise far more costly. Even so, the slower boarding time of an OPO bus meant that the frequency was still worse than before conversion. From late 1972, the number of buses on a route was actually increased at OPO conversion.

Experiments were carried out on DMS 240 in Chiswick Works from November 1971. It carried an all-red livery with yellow entrance doors and tried out two-leaf instead of four-leaf doors. It entered service in October 1973 at West Ham and the modifications were subsequently included in later batches.

Early 1972 saw a lull in OPO conversions, but on 13th May routes N85 and N86 became the first OPO night services, when Fleetlines took over.

Even before DMS 1 had entered service, a massive order for 1600 more had been placed for delivery in 1972-74. LT wanted 600 new buses per year to replace all RTs, RMs and RMLs by 1978. The initial plan was for 880 bodies by Park Royal and 720 by Metro-Cammell-Weymann, but in the end the split was 850/750. DMS/DM 368-1217 were built by Park Royal, while MCW built DMS/DM 1218-1967. The neat numbering division meant that high-numbered MCW buses arrived alongside low-numbered Park Royal vehicles. MCW used their own construction methods but conformed closely to LT's original design, apart from minor features, such as the shape of rain deflector strips and the front roof dome beading.

The original order specified 850 Leyland engines and 750 Gardner, but after production delays at Gardner the Leyland share was increased. A third possible engine was the Rolls-Royce Eagle, which was tried on DMS 864 and DM 1199, hence the schoolboy who could claim to come to school in a Daimler with a Rolls-Royce engine. After trials, LT considered the Rolls-Royce unit an acceptable alternative to Leyland and Gardner, although fuel consumption was high. This large order for 1600 began to arrive in April 1972, but British Leyland soon decided to move Fleetline production from Daimler's Coventry works to Farington factory. At first, no changes were made to Fleetline design, but the move inevitably caused a serious delay to delivery. The first Farington DMS was DMS 742, delivered in September 1973. Chassis codes for the 1600 buses were 2DM for Gardner and 3DM for Leyland buses, with odd minor variations. Gardner engines were fitted to DMS/DM 368-494, 608-611, 617-9, 637-639, 655, 659, 660, 1248-1371 and 1452-67. The remainder had Leyland engines. DMS 854 was the prototype B20, coded 3DM3/5, and is described later. Original body classifications were DM3 for Park Royal and DM4 for MCW. Reverting to all-red livery, the first of the 1600 entered service on 17th June 1972 on routes 44, 46 and 295. DMSs 463-467 were in use at West Ham from September with experimental two-leaf doors.

In 1973 nearly 500 DMSs were delivered, 538-806 by Park Royal and 1381/3-1602 by MCW. From DMSs 580 and 1416 (except 1417) respectively, yellow entrance doors and solid white LT logos were introduced. A further change from 586 (except 595 and 596) and 1428 was a nearside destination blind alongside the route number. Park Royal DMSs of this batch were coded DM3/1 and MCWs were DM4/1.

Eleven vehicles, DMSs 586-94/7/8, were allocated to the Round London Sightseeing Tour from 1973. From then until 1978 the Tour was run by new Fleetlines, buses being changed every six months. Also in 1973, DMS 1332 was fitted with experimental hydraulic brakes. Much later, in 1976-77, DMSs 2161, 2162, 2170 and 2224 were similarly treated, all working from Turnham Green garage. DMS 1332 was withdrawn early, but was involved in various trials at Chiswick, including hydraulic throttle and door operation. In early 1973, DMSs 1373 and 1376-97 became the first Farebox DMSs at Croydon, where they replaced the XAs. Their AFC machines accepted the flat fare but gave no ticket — the body code was DM4/2.

1973 saw DMSs replacing Swifts, RFs, RTs, Merlins and Routemasters. A rare instance of double and single-deckers being scheduled together was on route 83, shared between DMSs and SMSs on Sundays. In June, Hornchurch (RD) became LT's first garage without conductors.

Conversion of routes to one-person-operation had slowed down greatly and LT now saw that crew buses would be needed for some years. To maintain the flow of new buses, the 1974 order was altered to include 460 purpose-built conductor-operated DMs. Instead of an AFC machine, these had a bench seat for three. Thus DMs seated 71, plus five standing. As a stop-gap measure, 105 ordinary DMSs were put into service with conductors. Their AFC cabinets were retained but without equipment and cordoned off, while the 'Pay As You Enter' notices were changed to 'Please Pay the Conductor'. The crew DMSs were 745-784 at Cricklewood for route 16, and 785-90 and 1548-1572 at Muswell Hill and Potters Bar for the long 134, all from 15th December 1973. Route 149 was also included from 2nd February 1974, with DMSs 1595-1610 at Stamford Hill and 805-817 and 1611-15 at Edmonton.

From 10th May route 10 began a three-month experiment to increase usage of AFC machines (SMS route 227 was also involved). As already mentioned, boarding times on one-man buses were giving cause for concern and creating a need for more scheduled buses than expected. To publicise the AFC facility, the rear half only of the entrance door on the vehicles involved in the experiment was painted yellow, the front half being painted red. Leaflets and posters asked passengers to use the AFC side if they had the right money.

The first DMs entered service on 14th September 1974 on route 16, replacing the temporary crew DMSs. The DMs were numbered 918-1247 and 1703-1832. By the end of 1974, some 1000 Park Royal DM/Ss had been delivered, and DM 1000 was handed over in a small ceremony at Park Royal. The only OPO conversion of 1975 was route 183 on 4th January. For several years LT had had a severe shortage of serviceable buses, worsened by difficulties in obtaining spare parts. The Fleetline had by now a poor reliability record due to a number of factors, many of them related to LT's variation from standard Daimler design and inflexible maintenance procedures. The weight of the DMS (two tons more than an RML) put a great strain on components. The engine and gearbox suffered frequent over-heating and failure and the restricted engine compartment had a poor air-flow.

In 1974, Leyland altered its gearbox design, which caused problems with gears slipping and created a desperate reliability problem. The nadir was reached in February 1975, when Walworth's route 45 gained 27 new DMs: within 12 weeks, half the allocation was unfit for service! The situation gradually improved, but London Transport was disenchanted enough to look at potential successors. These included the MCW/Scania Metropolitan, the Leyland B15, and the futuristic XRM, which Chiswick's own designers were drawing up.

On the XRM, LT hoped to omit the gearbox completely to allow a low floor and side engine. The engine would drive a pump, supplying fluid to turbines in the rear wheel hubs. This was known as 'hydrostatic' drive. This ambitious notion was tried on DM 1787, rebuilt in 1976-77. It was extensively tested at Chiswick, but performance and fuel consumption were very poor, so the project was quietly forgotten. It was reclassified D 1787, regained its gearbox and went to Uxbridge in 1981, but was withdrawn in August 1982 after only 18 months' service. Clearly too fresh to waste, it was overhauled — the only Standard D to be done.

The DM was meant as a modern crew bus which could be converted to OPO if circumstances changed. However, the first few months showed that DMs were slow in operation due to opening and closing the doors at each stop. Despite this, two of the busiest crew services, the 24 and 29, were converted from RML to DM from 19th October and 14th December 1975 respectively. The 29 route kept DMs until 1977 and the 24 until 1979.

Back in March 1974, another large order was placed for 679 Fleetlines, for delivery in 1975-76, to clear the remaining Merlins and RTs. The first 279 buses, DMSs 1968-2246, were the last 'Standard' DMSs and introduced many features, including fire extinguishers, two-leaf doors, fluorescent blind box lighting and pantograph wipers. The 'Daimler' badge was now omitted from the bonnet, as the vehicle was now officially a 'Leyland Fleetline'.

This batch also brought a new livery with white upper deck window surrounds and yellow entrance doors. This attractive scheme, tried on DMS 46 in 1974, was deleted on repaint but lasted into 1988 on trainers. DMS 2121 arrived with the orange/brown seat moquette later adopted for Ms and Ts.

This '1975-76' order was actually delivered in 1976-78. Of the 279 Standards, Park Royal built 2058-2166. DMSs 2038-2057 and 2128-2246 had Gardner engines. DMS/DM 2247-2646, to a modified design, are described later. London Transport announced in 1976 that this was the last order for Fleetlines. The first of the new order arrived in February 1976. They replaced Merlins, Swifts, RTs and RFs.

DMS 1333 at London Bridge in 1974 shows another brief, and largely unsuccessful, campaign aimed at encouraging use of the AFC turnstile.
Capital Transport

DM 1185 newly into service on route 29 in December 1975, with Centre Point in the background.
Colin Stannard

The look of DMSs and DMs was considerably improved by the introduction of white relief around the upper deck windows, as seen on DMS 2218 at Uxbridge. Capital Transport

Deliveries of Standards continued into June 1977, overlapping with early B20s. The exceptionally hot summer of 1976 caused many engine seizures. Four more Rolls-Royce engines were purchased in 1976, being fitted to DMSs 1968, 2059, 2120 with one spare.

Meanwhile, by 1976 the Certificates of Fitness of earlier Fleetlines were about to expire, and overhauls had to be considered. LT had intended to give DMSs regular overhauls at Aldenham Works in the usual Aldenham way: bodywork lifted off the chassis and both stripped down and repaired separately.

As a pilot, DMS 1 entered Aldenham in April 1976, but serious problems were encountered and it did not reappear until March 1977. Even then it had to return for further waterproofing. By an oversight, nobody had told Park Royal to make its bodies detachable until it was too late: separation caused distortion. To overhaul DMSs, Aldenham was therefore remodelled to handle whole vehicles.

Another pilot overhaul was done on DMS 118; then production overhauls began in July 1977. Overhauled DMSs all emerged with all-red livery, pull-in front windows and 'pantograph' nearside windscreen wipers following an experiment with these on some vehicles at West Ham garage. The offside wipers kept to the old design, even on the last Fleetlines.

Overhauls speeded up in 1978 and a pilot MCW overhaul was carried out on DMS 1449. Body-lifting was possible on MCW Fleetlines, but this would need a

A Park Royal bodied DMS undergoing overhaul in Aldenham Works, September 1978. Though Metro-Cammell vehicles were capable of body and chassis separation without distortion, they were overhauled in the same way. Capital Transport

new production line and so at first it was decided not to overhaul MCW vehicles. A total of 161 Fleetlines were overhauled up to the end of 1978. The process was then stopped as LT began selling off the class.

In March 1977 DMSs which looked and sounded very different from earlier examples arrived at Bexleyheath. The final 400 London Fleetlines were all of this type, often referred to by the Leyland designation 'B20'. The origins of the B20 go back to January 1971 when DMS 88 was rebuilt as an experiment in noise-reduction: the engine air vents were moved up onto the sides of the cosmetic shrouds. DMS 88 was tested before entering service in November 1971 at Shepherds Bush: it kept these features until withdrawal.

The next step was a redesigned rear end incorporating the raised air intakes. The famous angled air vents on each side of the rear window were designed and a mock-up set fitted to DMS 1665 in 1974.

The first true B20 was DMS 854 which was rebuilt by Leyland. As well as the angled vents, this bus received a turbocharged Leyland engine and new engine compartment layout, all to reduce noise and a wide-angle lens in the lower deck back window to maintain rear vision. The turbocharger caused the bonnet to be extended slightly and encouraged overheating. Nevertheless, DMS 854 arrived in its new form in late 1975 and spent the following year on test, finally creeping into service in 1977. It was withdrawn in 1983 and eventually sold to Hong Kong.

DMS 2364 appears to have had some trouble during delivery from the Park Royal factory to Aldenham in February 1977, affording this view of the engine compartment. It was one of the B20s to enter service at Bexleyheath starting the following month. Capital Transport

Anticipating new legislation on noise levels, a noble but expensive option, London Transport ordered DMSs 2247-2526 and DMs 2527-2646 as B20s, and they arrived in London throughout 1977 and the first half of 1978. All had turbocharged Leyland engines. DMSs 2247-2346 were bodied by MCW and coded 3DM8, while the rest were built at Park Royal and classified 3DM6 for DMSs, or 3DM6/1 for DMs. At Bexleyheath the B20 quickly proved more unreliable than the 'Standard' DMS, and older Standard vehicles had to be sent in as back-up.

One instantly-recognisable B20 was Stockwell's DMS 2478, which was allocated to the Round London Sightseeing Tour from October 1977. The upper deck was painted white as an advert for Air India. This attractive livery survived until September 1980.

Meanwhile, DM operation on the busy 29, which had been introduced in December 1975, was proving inefficient. On 19th March 1977, these DMs were swapped with RMs on the more suburban 141. Still hoping to use DMs permanently on crew work, LT decided to try increasing circulating space by removing the front nearside bench seat. The result would resemble a DMS with AFC removed, so DMSs 854 and 2488 promptly lost their machines. They went into crew use on route 24 although 854 was rarely seen. The modification did little to improve boarding times.

Park Royal delivered their last DMS in November 1977 and switched to DMs. Metro-Cammell DMS delivery continued to arrive up to February 1978. The same month, on the 26th, saw the start of a massive Multi-ride scheme in the Havering area; a previous trial at Wood Green had involved flat-fare routes only, but this

One instantly-recognisable B20 was DMS 2478, allocated to the Round London Sightseeing Tour from October 1977 and moved to Palmers Green garage the following year. Its red and white wrap-round advert for Air India survived until September 1980. Capital Transport

was much more ambitious, including all routes in the area; it was hoped that Multi-ride could make OPO fast enough for trunk services. Most of the buses involved were DMSs, and these gained cancelling equipment as at Wood Green. This promising scheme was very popular with passengers but did not achieve its aim of providing a substantial improvement in boarding times.

London Transport's last new Fleetline arrived on 23rd August 1978: DM 2646 spent much of the following year in Shillibeer 1829 green/cream livery celebrating 150 years of buses in London. Even at this late stage, some of the DM family's problems had not been solved. Gearboxes and brakes failed much earlier on DMSs than other types. DMS rear brake linings lasted 6-8 weeks, compared to 6 months on an RM. Other problems were structural weakness, fuel and water leaks and steering problems. All this pushed up DMS maintenance bills far enough to outweigh the wages saved by converting to OPO.

The first Metrobuses and Titans had already been delivered and 1000 were ordered for 1978-80. This would allow Fleetline withdrawals to begin. It was said that a DMS cost 25% more in fuel and maintenance than a Metrobus or Titan. The best Park Royal DMSs would be kept, but others would be sold, either for scrap or further service. As we shall see, LT's preferences for certain sub-groups of DMS would alter several times.

On 26th February 1979, DMS 251 was the first member of the class to be disposed of by London Transport when it was sold for scrap, although less than eight years old. The stock of London's Fleetlines had been intact for just six months (barring one vehicle which had been destroyed by fire but not formally withdrawn).

The first reversion of a DMS route to crew operation occurred on 31st March 1979 when the 106 (Hackney and Tottenham garages) regained RMs. Soon more routes saw the return of conductors. Another milestone came on 27th May 1979, when LT abandoned its troublesome Automatic Fare Collection machinery. The AFC entrance was roped off and all passengers had to pay the driver. This change of heart, plus the slowness of crew operated doored buses, prompted LT to convert DM 2577 to be suitable for crew or OPO use. It received barriers to direct passengers past the driver, brackets for ticket machines and flip-over 'Pay Driver/Pay Conductor' plates on the front of the bus and on the cab door. Many other DMs followed. Early conversions kept their DM numbers, but from June 1980 they were reclassified D. Four DMSs were also given flipover plates to allow dual use — 2279, 2286 and 2287 at Brixton were altered in this way in August 1981, when doored crew buses were needed for route N87. These were unofficially given DS classifications. The fourth was Golden Jubilee DS 1933 at Thornton Heath.

Removal of Fleetlines from service began in earnest on 18th March 1979, when Fulwell garage received its first Metrobuses. Within a few months, Fulwell was the first garage to lose its entire DMS allocation. The first DM disposed of was DM 1757 in October 1979, two months after being deroofed at Finsbury Park railway bridge. This was the only DM sold in 1979. A total of 357 DMSs were deleted from stock during the year.

The last Fleetline for London, DM 2646 seen at Muswell Hill, was repainted in a special livery in 1979 to commemorate the 150th anniversary of Shillibeer's introduction of bus services in London. It had entered service the previous year. Mike Harris

DMS 340, working from Battersea garage and seen at Victoria, was an early recipient of T-shape advertising, which required the roundel to be squeezed in behind the driver's cab window. Rothman was the biggest client for this new idea when it was first introduced. G.A. Rixon

Not all withdrawn DMSs were sold. London Transport realised they would make good driver trainers, and in 1979 DMS 69 was converted as such. During 1980 a further 40 followed. New features included a seat for the instructor, five extra mirrors, an instructor's hand brake and internal indicator lights.

Several garages lost their whole Fleetline allocation in 1980/81, with Metrobuses taking over in the north and west and Titans in east and south London. There were also more reversions to RM and many more DMs converted to D. By the end of 1981, LT had just 1173 DMS, 266 DM and 194 D.

To cover Certificate expiries, newly overhauled vehicles were brought into Croydon and fitted with fareboxes for the flat-fare routes: they could be identified for flat fare use only by a white 'C' on the front offside window pillar.

In 1980 it was decided to keep the Fleetline longer because of vehicle shortages. Recertifications were carried out on both MCW and PRV buses and overhauls restarted on Park Royal DMSs. This policy altered in 1981, when Park Royal overhauls were abandoned, and overhauls began on the MCW batch DMS 1833-1967 instead! Running alongside was a preference to keep Leyland-engined buses instead of Gardner, mainly for standardisation, though also because of the Leyland engine's better heating.

The first work for most of the final DM deliveries was from Stockwell garage on route 168 and the Round London Sightseeing Tour. DM 2633 crosses Waterloo Bridge. Capital Transport

As fewer crew-operated vehicles were now needed, no pre-B20 DMs/Ds would be overhauled (except D 1787 already mentioned). When a D was sold, its OPO equipment was transferred to another DM. After DMS 1967, overhauls began on the Leyland-engined batch 1969-2037. Despite their poor reliability, the entire B20 fleet was to be kept in service, and May 1981 saw DMS 2351 enter Aldenham for a pilot overhaul. This was successful and production overhauls of B20s began in late 1981. Aldenham started to concentrate on these and work on 'Standards' slowed down.

New PSV regulations were to start in January 1983, requiring every bus to pass an annual Freedom From Defect examination. This change caused some indecision at 55 Broadway. The first effect was to give each bus an annual light overhaul at its own garage, backed up by a full overhaul at Aldenham every four years. Aldenham overhauls of pre-B20 Fleetlines would cease entirely. DMS 1987 was the last to enter Aldenham on 22nd December 1981 and the last to be outshopped was DMS 1857 on 24th May 1982. As 1982 began, Aldenham was concentrating on B20s.

Then a further policy change took place. The B20 type would only be needed for about four years, so works overhauls of them too could end: DMS 2374 was the last into Aldenham on 26th July 1982, and the last to leave the Works was DMS 2317 on 3rd December 1982. A repaint programme began in late 1982, some of the first to benefit being the DMs used on the Round London Sightseeing Tour.

LT was able to stop DMS overhauls because it was taking them out of service at a furious rate. Large numbers of new Ms and Ts were arriving, while few RMs were being withdrawn, and services were massively cut after the Greater London Council's low-fares policy ended in September 1982. At that time, some 220 standard Fleetlines were withdrawn in just a few weeks! 1982-3 saw the scheduled total of Fleetlines fall from 1048 to just 305. Twenty garages were cleared of all their DMSs. Bexleyheath went from 100% DMS to having none at all. The aim was to remove all crew-operated and pre-B20 Fleetlines, and concentrate the remainder at Wandle District garages in south London.

The 'Standard' pre-B20 Fleetline was withdrawn in droves during 1982 and 1983. When new Ms and Ts replaced B20s, the latter were cascaded to replace Standards at other garages. By the end of 1983, the only Standards left in service were ten at New Cross, two at Holloway, two at Croydon and one at Thornton Heath. The crew-operated DM was phased out, the last being DMs 2548 and 2552 at Westbourne Park, which last carried conductors on route 18 on 19th September 1983. However, eight DMs had been put on the Round London Sightseeing Tour in 1982, from Victoria, and they survived a little longer. 1982/3 saw a real attempt to clear derelict/cannibalised vehicles from the fleet list, including several hundred already sold to Ensign but not yet recorded as such.

The abundance of surplus Fleetlines had an impact on driver-training. In 1982 most of the existing DMS trainers were inspected and many withdrawn. Four much newer pre-B20s (though unoverhauled) were converted into trainers: DMS 2168, 2181, 2186 and 2187. In late 1983 overhauled Standards began to come out of service, and some of them became trainers. The only DMS to become an LT staff bus was DMS 2177, which went onto the Aylesbury–Aldenham run in 1983. It was transferred to Bus Engineering Ltd in 1985. When Aldenham closed in 1986 it was made redundant, but later became an exhibition bus for the London Borough of Haringey.

DMS 2172 was involved in a fire at Catford in September 1980 and lay disused for over a year, but in 1982 it was stripped to the bare chassis, shortened to make it easier to handle and was used for mechanical training before being sold to Paddington Technical College.

The front portion of withdrawn DM 963 was removed in 1982 and installed as an exhibit in the London Transport Museum. It remained there until the Museum was rebuilt in 1993. DM 948 was taken into Aldenham in October 1982 as a conversion for export to the Far East. After a change of heart, the bus was converted to open-top. DM 1102 was similarly rebuilt in 1983 and repainted white with yellow doors. Both vehicles were transferred to the Sales Department for use as demonstrators.

Another experiment was the Maxwell gearbox, which was experimentally fitted into Croydon's DMS 2205 in 1983: this bus was to outlive all other Standards. DMS 1967 was fitted with electronic diagnostic equipment, but left service in December 1983. It was then used to train staff on BUSCO radio, ending up on ordinary training duties from February 1987. DM 2559 after withdrawal in 1983 was converted into a Mobile Survey Control vehicle, with office upstairs and a generator downstairs. It was also repainted, uniquely retaining white window frames, and was transferred into the Service Vehicle fleet.

At New Cross, Ds 1062 and 1063 received white waistbands (1062 was briefly adopted as a showbus). D 1063 lost the waistband but gained white diagonal stripes as a promotional livery for the Bus & Coach Council, part of a national campaign against the Government's plans for nationwide bus privatisation.

Four Fleetlines were involved in London Transport's Golden Jubilee celebrations in 1983. DMS 1933 at Thornton Heath was magnificently painted into prewar LT livery as a dual OPO/crew bus (hence now known as DS 1933). It also gained a 'Daimler' front badge and windscreen slipboards instead of a flipover plate. D 2629 at Croydon, celebrating both 50 years of LT and 100 years of the Borough of Croydon, gained brown/white Croydon Corporation Tramways livery and was nicknamed 'The Chocolate Box'. It was repainted red in July 1985. It then donated body parts to the Arsenal Football Museum for a mock-up of DMS 2291. The third jubilee bus was DMS 2593, which gained a gold waistband and worked at various Wandle garages. Finally, Ensign's former DMS 1682 was painted into 1933 livery, renumbered DF 1682, and worked on the London tours.
G.A. Rixon

As 1984 started, London Transport removed the last Standards (except 2205) from service. Holloway's pair of pre-B20s were withdrawn in January, while Croydon's DMS 2017 last saw passenger service on 4th February. The ten at New Cross were more slowly evicted, the last four being put into store on 21st February. Even then D 1143 re-entered service at New Cross for one day in March. Thornton Heath's showbus DS 1933 ceased regular service on 5th March but reappeared occasionally, lastly on Wimbledon Tennis specials in June. It was then withdrawn. Now only experimental DMS 2205 at Croydon was left.

The next step was to remove Fleetlines from garages outside Wandle District, including Catford in January 1984, Wandsworth on 21st March and Chalk Farm in October. The last DMSs outside Wandle were 20 at Holloway, which last ran in February 1985.

On 29th June 1984, the London Transport Executive was replaced by London Regional Transport. LRT found itself with a surplus of DMSs and found work for them from the summer on crew services 2B, 77A, 88, 109 and 133. DMS 1 was donated to the London Transport Museum where it joined other vehicles in long-term store.

The two open-top DMs were borrowed from Sales by Catford for the new Thames Barrier Shuttle which began on 25th May 1984. DM 1102 kept its white livery until February 1985. Then DM 948 was given the name 'MV Royal Eagle' and DM 1102 'MV Royal Daffodil'. They have run there each summer.

A week later, the DMs on the Round London Sightseeing Tour were taken out of service. Some were converted to OPO, some went to Holloway as spares for crew use, and the rest were sent to Battersea and Camberwell for private hire and tour work.

In 1984 LT decided to keep its B20 DMSs until the late 1980s. This meant that 189 B20s which had not been overhauled would now be dealt with. In September, DMS 2248 and D 2583 entered Aldenham as pilots, and the main programme started with DMS 2464 in January 1985. However, Aldenham only carried out 20 of the overhauls, considering them uneconomic. The rest were overhauled under contract by Leyland, Eastern Coach Works and Midland Red.

London Buses Ltd, formed on 1st April 1985, also overhauled 73 DMSs itself between then and February 1986; mechanical work was done at the home garage, bodywork repairs were carried out at local garages and repaints were done at Aldenham or at Clapham. This was another attempt to reduce overhaul costs. Slight expansion, the first in seven years, occurred in 1985. The year started with 551 Fleetlines in stock, and 253 scheduled for service. In April DM 2643 appeared from overhaul with new seating and went to Camberwell for private hire and tour duties. A few months later it gained a broad white band with Selkent Travel fleetnames.

Ogle Designs had borrowed withdrawn DMS 1887 in 1983 to review bus interior design for LT. In 1984 DMS 2456 went into Chiswick to be rebuilt to their modified design. It emerged in early 1985 radically altered. The entrance area was much more spacious, with a split step. High-visibility green handrails were used for the first time. Inside the bus, the AFC unit and divided gangway were swept away and circulating space was much improved. A long, straight staircase was fitted on the offside, and the exit doorway was moved forward to line up with it. The exit also gained an extra shallow step. The seating capacity ended up as H41/23D. The cab was also redesigned, with a new instrument panel and accessible controls under the steering wheel (DMS 2377 received a similar cab design). DMS 2456 re-entered service as a crew-operated bus on route 77 from Stockwell in early 1985, moving to the 88 in February 1986: it was restricted to crew use because a ticket machine could not be fitted to the rounded cab. This problem was solved by April 1988, when the bus appeared in OPO service for the first time on route 77A. It later moved to Brixton as an OPO bus.

For many years an old London bus had been used by the Metropolitan Police Training College, Hendon. DMS 1621 was loaned there from August 1984 and was officially sold to the College in January 1986.

By the start of 1986, nearly all London Fleetlines were B20s, capable of OPO, and running in Wandle District. The only exceptions were DMs 2641-3, used for private hire work at Camberwell, and pre-B20 DMS 2205 at Croydon. Short-lived livery standardisation was achieved on 14th January 1986, when DMS 2486 at Stockwell was the last in service in the old red and white colours.

London Buses' priorities were very different from those of the old London Transport Executive. Making maximum use of vehicles was now more important than standardisation; this was to revive the Fleetline's fortunes in 1986-88. First, it was declared that the B20 was a 'useful vehicle' and would be kept in service for another five years; no routine withdrawals occurred. In January 1986, 311 DMSs/Ds were scheduled for service as follows: Brixton (8), Croydon (64), Elmers End (14), Merton (63), Stockwell (55), Sutton (62) and Thornton Heath (45). A total of 490 Fleetlines were in stock. Over the summer of 1986, all OPO vehicles received cab assault screens.

The year 1987 started with 488 Fleetlines in stock. By this time almost all garages had ceased using side blinds, and a start had been made on painting or panelling over the disused box. DMS 2313 at Stockwell received vandal-proof plastic seats at the back of the upstairs saloon. In March DMs 2641-2643 were replaced at Camberwell by Titans, and were immediately converted into Ds.

In spring 1987 London Buses Ltd won a tendered network in the Kingston area, to be run by Norbiton garage. To cut costs, Norbiton's Metrobus fleet would be partly replaced by Fleetlines resurrected from the training fleet. This plan caused much surprise, especially as the trainers were all 'Standards' which LT had spent years eradicating. The best 35 trainers were sent to Chiswick, Leyland, Kent Engineering and Ensign: all were Leylands and all but seven had MCW bodies. They were refurbished and emerged advert-free. This was the first groups of DMSs to lose its redundant AFC units in favour of luggage pens. All were painted red with yellow doors, but DMS 2006 partly retained its training livery.

The initial Norbiton fleet consisted of DMSs 678, 711, 714, 717, 719, 819, 1426, 1447, 1473, 1477, 1488, 1500, 1511, 1537, 1626, 1837, 1852, 1859, 1862, 1867, 1873, 1884, 1889, 1890, 1900, 1901, 1904, 1936, 1950, 1990, 1993, 2006, 2008, 2103 and D 1804 (which still carried the number DM 1804).

The start of the new contracts was on 27th June 1987, when nine DMSs were in use. The rest filtered in over following weeks, mixing with Ms on routes 71, 85 and 213. DMSs were less common on the 65 because of the low entrance to Kingston garage (hence a 'No Entrance For DMS Vehicles' sign). In 1988, DMS 1985 joined the NB fleet and the name KINGSTON BUS was adopted.

In August 1987, DMS 2281 at Croydon was a herald of things to come, being fitted experimentally with a new Iveco engine. Another experiment was with DMS 2405 which entered service the same month with a dot-matrix rear route number display. On route 194B, it displayed '194' and 'B' alternately!

From 31st October 1987, London Buses won three services on contract from Surrey County Council, providing new work for Sutton DMSs as far out as Gatwick Airport.

DMS 2456 after conversion to Ogle Designs recommendations was easily recognisable by the layout of the offside lower deck windows, revised panelling being necessary for the straight staircase installed. It is seen at Hyde Park Corner. Mike Harris

More general developments in 1987 included the debut of the new red/white/grey London Buses livery and redesigned roundel: both soon spread. The Leaside District livery with white waistband and black skirt was also applied to several Leaside DMS trainers. The year also saw the spread of the bulky Wayfarer electronic ticket machine.

In November 1987, more Croydon Fleetlines began to receive Iveco engines. Some 100 were to be re-engined, almost the entire allocation of TC and A in 1987-8. By replacing worn-out Leyland units by modern engines, LBL hoped to ensure another five years of service from its Fleetlines. The re-engined buses were recognisable because the nearside 'chimney' was panelled over and a new air intake grille inserted in the nearside wall of the engine compartment (back to the pre-B20 layout!). When first converted, the Iveco engines had a loud scream on pulling away, but they quietened down when the turbochargers were better treated. Iveco Fleetlines were recoded 5DM6, the last new engineering code to be allocated.

The end of 1987 saw another clear-out as disused Fleetlines were sold off to leave just the PSV fleet and about 40 trainers. All five B20 trainers (DMS 2396, 2410, 2478, 2505, D 2580) were restored to service. Older Fleetlines, some in very poor condition, took their place as trainers. Derelict DMS 1499 was sent to Norbiton as a source of spare parts (as BX was later to acquire DMSs 2100 and 2158). Chiswick also transformed D 1159 into a mobile office in white livery. The front doorway was panelled over and a diesel generator mounted next to the cab.

The 'Norbiton exercise' was seen as a success, and London Buses took the same idea further from 16th January 1988 with 'Bexleybus', the unit which took over Bexleyheath garage and a batch of tendered routes. Bexleybus had a bold cream and blue livery and its own fleet number system. So 17 derelict DMSs were chosen, and, incredibly, LBL repurchased 14 Fleetlines from Clydeside Scottish.

All 31 were overhauled and repainted by Ensign. DMSs 2063, 2064, 2068, 2074, 2108, 2109, 2110, 2112, 2118, 2121, 2125, 2143, 2156, 2166, Ds 1146, 1160, and 1195 were numbered Bexleybus 91-100/4-7/1-3 in that order. Front blind boxes were rebuilt for two-piece displays, while side/rear ones were painted over. The first bus finished was DMS 2166, which received fleet number 2166 for publicity photos and kept it for a time. The 14 ex-Clydeside buses had all been rebuilt as single-door, with one-window front blind-boxes and extra indicator lights. They had been DMSs 1492, 1580, 1610, 1649, 1656, 1657, 1669, 1670, 1671, 1679, 1683, 1686, 1687 and 2021 and were now numbered 77-90 respectively. A complication with Bexleybus was the 'Autocheck' pass-checking system being tried there. All buses were fitted with a small reader each side of the entrance. The Clydeside buses ended up seating H44/31F, except No.90, which was H44/28F. The others were upseated to H45/27D. 'Autocheck' stickers also appeared on the fronts of buses. All Bexleybus Fleetlines ran without the cosmetic rear bonnet-shrouds.

London Buses' old banger acquisitions were not extended. However, the DMS family was at last in efficient use, with 386 scheduled for service out of 490 in stock. January 1988 saw Croydon's last ten DMSs re-engined by Iveco. This left Gardner-engined DMS 2205 very much out of place and it departed on 27th January for Brixton, where it was more at home among other experimentals. Then a start was made on re-engining Sutton's Fleetlines. One bus per day was converted at a workshop in New Cross, continuing into the spring.

Bexleybus liveried D 1146 at Bexleyheath shopping centre in April 1988. Mike Harris

DMS 2291 reappeared in February, rebuilt as an open-topper after being deroofed in August 1987. The work was done by Kent Engineering and allowed the vehicle to be used for private hire and training. It was upseated to O44/28D with waterproof seats and floor upstairs. Public address and radio were fitted. Leaside livery was applied as the vehicle was based at Stamford Hill. Its first use in service was on Monday 30th May 1988 on commercial service 310B. It then became the regular vehicle on summer leisure route 333. In 1988 it also performed a goodwill visit to Rotterdam and Den Haag.

Another autonomous unit was planned for Sutton, using existing DMSs and Ds. In March 1988, experimental liveries appeared on DMS 2409 (red/white/black) and DMS 2487 (red/white/maroon). From 24th August, D 2589 appeared in final prototype livery, with beige skirt and yellow waistband, 'Suttonbus' fleet name and garage phone number on the front. LBL was anxious not to unveil the new livery prematurely and restored D 2589 to standard after a brief inspection. By then DMS 2368 was Sutton's only non-Iveco vehicle.

The Suttonbus scheme finally began on 26th November 1988, with buses at the garage receiving the red/yellow/beige livery.

In October 1987, London Buses won three services on contract from Surrey County Council, taking Sutton DMSs out to Epsom (508), Walton-on-Hill (520) and Gatwick (522). These became part of the Suttonbus operation when it was set up the following year. Mike Harris

At the end of 1988, the following garages of London Buses were operating Fleetlines:

Bexleyheath: Routes 96, 99, 178, 229, 269, 272, 401, 469 and 472 (Sats).
Brixton: Routes 59, 95, 109 (Sats) and 133.
Croydon: Routes 50, 68, 75 (Suns), 130 and X30, 166 and 190 (Suns).
Merton: Routes 44, 49 (Suns), 57, 77, 155, 156 (Suns), 219 and 280.
Norbiton: Routes 65, 71, 85, 213.
Stockwell: Routes 37, 77A, 88 (Suns), 156 and 170.
Sutton: Routes 80, 93, 151, 152, 154, 157, 163, 164, 522 and Tesco free bus.
Thornton Heath: 59, 60, 64, 109, 194B, 264 and 389.

When London Buses' subsidiaries took control at the end of the year, Selkent took Bexleyheath; while Brixton, Croydon and Thornton Heath were under South London Transport; Merton, Stockwell and Sutton were run by London General; and Norbiton came under the wing of London United Busways.

After the modest expansion of the previous two years, 1989 saw stability for the London Fleetline. Fitting of new Iveco engines continued, so that Croydon, Sutton and Thornton Heath were totally converted by August.

On 16th April, Autocheck trials ended, and Bexleybus vehicles had the machines removed, causing an increase in seating capacity. Mid-1989 also saw many DMSs being fitted with a luggage pen instead of Automatic Fare Collection machines (10 years after AFC use ended).

Despite Bexleybus's claims that Fleetlines could be run as reliably as RTs, after only 18 months use the 31 DMSs began to depart, the first being delicensed in August. This slow process continued into 1990.

During 1989 there was a lot of DMS activity in the area of special services and specialised vehicles. Finchley's trainer DMS 2168 was back into passenger service for a rail-replacement service in February and again in July, having gained a tachograph. Stamford Hill's open-top DMS 2291 was scheduled for the summer Leisure Bus 333. On Sunday 28th May it was hired by Arsenal football team to celebrate their FA Cup victory; during the celebration, the bus had its windscreen smashed! For its 1989 operation on the Thames Barrier service, Plumstead's open toppers were repainted red with grey skirt and white upper deck panels and SELKENT TRAVEL fleetnames.

Developments in 1990 began on 6th January, when two-thirds of Norbiton's Fleetlines were replaced by surplus Metrobuses. Surprisingly, four of the Norbiton buses immediately re-entered service at Merton, the first Standards there for seven years! The four buses were DMSs 1447, 1890 and 2008 and D 1804, which finally carried its correct classification. They were used mostly on routes 44 and 219.

Withdrawals of pre-B20s from Norbiton and Bexleyheath were under way, but the B20 Fleetline was still largely intact. Iveco engines were now fitted in 201 of them.

Late 1989 and early 1990 witnessed great vehicle problems at Bexleyheath, resulting in any bus going into service on any route. Titans completely replaced Fleetlines there by March, the last DMS in use being No.91 (DMS 2063).

The Metropolitan Police School at Hendon gained disused Bexleybus DMS 1657 in January. In March the first few DMSs appeared with the new rear light clusters which were to become common. The unique DMS 2205 at Brixton was transferred to the training fleet in April, and lost its experimental Maxwell gearbox and Gardner engine in favour of a standard gearbox and Leyland engine.

Displaying a very shabby image is DMS 2006 towards the end of its career with the Kingston Bus unit. Gerald Mead

Somewhat smarter is D 2564 (showing DMS 2564) in LBL corporate livery at the time of Stockwell's takeover of route 196 when London Buses regained the route in April 1990. Gerald Mead

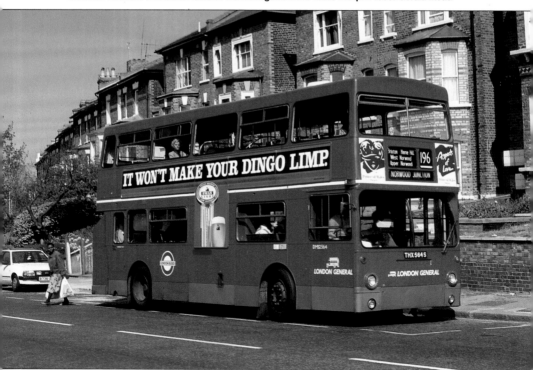

In 1990, London United trainers DMS 1426 and DMS 1537 at Stamford Brook received white and grey bands and 'Riverside Bus' fleetnames. These were removed after about a year.

Four withdrawn Bexleybus DMSs were put back into service in April. Full repaints were not worthwhile, so they kept Bexleybus cream and blue, with full LBL red livery applied at the front, presenting a very shabby image. The four buses were D 1160 and DMSs 2109, 2112 and 2143, which ran from Merton for a short time.

21st July 1990 brought tendering upheaval in south London. Streatham regained DMSs after a six-year gap, while Brixton became all-DMS apart from three Dennis Dominators. At the same time, Merton's last pre-B20s (Ds 1160, 1804, DMSs 1889, 1890, 2008, 2109, 2112 and 2143) were withdrawn, the four ex-Bexleybus vehicles being included. Norbiton's DMS allocation was reduced to just DMSs 719 and 1873, which were removed in August, ending the three-year revival there. Suttonbus as a separate identity was also on the way out, as new applications of that livery ceased in August.

In late September 1990, surplus Metrobuses were available, and London Buses was at last ready to begin withdrawal of B20 Fleetlines. Merton received its first few Ms and more arrived over the following months. The first few withdrawals of B20s were converted for driver-training.

DMS 2143, one of four ex-Bexleybus vehicles pressed back into service elsewhere in spring 1990. It is seen at Clapham Junction in May. Mike Harris

The DMS entered 1991 having achieved 20 years in London, something which had seemed very unlikely back in 1978-9. However, this was the first year of major B20 withdrawals: 180 were sold that year, starting with the remaining Leyland-engined vehicles, and others became trainers.

The big event of 1991 was the Wandsworth revision of 25th May, with many routes becoming LT contracts. All these routes were DMS strongholds and now gained Ms. From the start of the year, spare Ms began to arrive at London General to start replacement. Sutton's first M started on 7th January and Stockwell's first (apart from experimental vehicles) on 24th January. Disused Fleetlines began to stack up at Fulwell and Walthamstow. The official changeover in May converted many long-standing DMS routes to Metrobus, including the 170, which had been worked by DMSs since 24th July 1971, nearly 20 years earlier! Stockwell and Streatham lost all their DMSs, but Merton kept a few.

Summer 1991 saw DMSs at just five garages (A, AL, BN, TC and TH). By the end of November, all but four of Brixton's DMSs had been replaced by Titans. Croydon too had gained many Ts and had only 19 licensed Fleetlines. Half of Sutton's allocation had been removed and only DMS 2406 was still active at Merton.

However, there were several Fleetline oddities of 1991 to excite the enthusiast. In January LT began its 'Supercar' advertising, featuring a remarkable rebuild of DMS 1515. The front two bays of bodywork were left, but the rest was stripped down to chassis level and replaced by a mock-up of part of a 1973 tube car and a Network SouthEast class 321 cab! The interiors were fully modelled, including a Piccadilly Line map. Ownership of the vehicle passed to London Underground.

Some areas of London which had long since given up DMSs saw them carrying passengers again in 1991. In April Leaside won some school contract work from the London Borough of Islington and decided to use four redundant B20s, DMSs 2266, 2321, 2324 and 2474, which arrived in May from Stockwell. After winning further contracts, trainers DMS 681 and D 1868 were prepared for a return to service at Stamford Hill in August. Stamford Hill also received Iveco DMS 2260 from Merton in August and 2247 in September.

Similarly, in July, London Northern had three trainers (Ds 2542, 2545 and 2595) approved for emergency private hire cover from Holloway, and East London acquired Merton's D 2600 in July. When East London took over schooldays-only route 345 from 25th November, it used staff and vehicles from the private hire department and 2600 was a regular performer.

Our story now enters 1992, the last year of regular DMS operation in London. For a class supposedly unpopular all its life, the DMS took a long time to disappear. Merton's DMS 2406 was last seen in use on 4th January. Merton had had nearly 21 years of continuous DMS operation, from 30th January 1971.

South London was due for another shake-up on 14th March, with Ms moving into Croydon and Ts into Thornton Heath. This cleared TH of Fleetlines and removed all but seven of Croydon's: TC kept DMSs 2375, 2411, 2438, 2445, 2480, 2494 and D 2633, restricted to routes 68, 130 and X30. April 1992 saw the removal of Sutton's once-large fleet. By mid-May only D 2646 (appropriately) was left: it was finally delicensed in June. Now Croydon was alone, with DMSs 2438, 2480 and 2494 still in daily use in July. D 2633 was withdrawn to become Croydon's private hire vehicle, being re-registered WLT916. DMSs 2480 and 2494 were taken to Fulwell in October.

That left only DMS 2438, which stayed in regular use throughout 1992, on routes 68 and 130. On 2nd January 1993, South London commemorated 22 years of the DMS and the end of regular operation by running a 'Londoner 459' round trip on

D 2600 was surprisingly allocated to North Street garage in July 1991 and allocated to the East London Coaches contract fleet, which allowed cameo appearances on school contract routes 345 (Chingford-Goodmayes) and 449 (County Park Estate-Romford). It is seen on the former route at Woodford Wells in May 1992. It also appeared on regular routes 129 and 174 following Titan shortages during February 1993. Upon sale it continued to transport schoolchildren, but for the John Penfold School in Harefield. Mike Harris

DMS 2438 from Chipstead Valley to Hammond Street, right across Greater London. The journey was successfully completed in 3½ hours. DMS 2438 returned to Croydon for occasional service, its last use being on 20th January on route 130. This was the end of ordinary operation with LBL Fleetlines. DMS 2438 itself had achieved 15 years of operation.

London Buses still had 28 B20s and nine Standards in stock. Eight of the 37 buses carried passengers. Leaside had DMS 681 and D 1868, London Northern had DMS 2168 and East London had D 2600 at North Street.

The open-top fleet comprised Selkent's DM 948 and DM 1102 for the Greenwich tourist service and Leaside's DMS 2291 for the Lea Valley leisure services. DMS 2291 also operated on ordinary routes, including crew use on route 73 on a few Saturdays in the summer of 1992. D 2556, converted to open-top at Coventry, was used on route Z1 in the summer of 1993.

The eighth passenger-carrier was South London's D 2633, used for hire work at Croydon until April 1993. It departed to Fulwell in May 1993.

The rest were driver-trainers, though these were mostly being replaced by early Titans and Metrobuses. London General however selected twelve B20 trainers which have been repainted in a new livery of red with yellow front and roof. These smart vehicles were unofficially reclassified DMT.

At the time London Buses was privatised in autumn 1994, four companies owned DMS type vehicles. Leaside had three DMSs, London General two DMSs and the 12 DMTs, London Northern had one DMS and one D and Selkent had two open-toppers, DMs 948 and 1102.

The shortlived predecessor of London Pride Sightseeing was Emmaheath Ltd, whose name was anonymous on vehicles but whose operation was nevertheless conspicuous in the fetching livery of white, orange and pink. DMS 1424 shows the shading as it crosses Trafalgar Square during July 1984. It later saw service with Ensignbus and had a short spell with New Enterprise Coaches of Tonbridge before reaching its last stop in the yard of PVS at Carlton. G.A. Rixon

SIGHTSEEING TOURS IN LONDON

The class have been the backbone of sightseeing tours within the Capital since the introduction of DMS 1256 in June 1979, paradoxically hired by London Transport to supplement the Tour, before settling down as a rain and breakdown relief vehicle on the normally open-topped summer route 74Z (Baker Street–London Zoo circular).

During the early eighties operations mushroomed; by 1985 nearly 100 Fleetlines were being utilised around the landmarks of London. These were operated by Ebdon's Tours, London Cityrama, London Pride, Maybury's Coaches (later London Sightseeing Tours) and LT themselves who augmented their DMs with hired DMSs from Crouch End Coaches and Ensign's contract fleet. Wealden Motor Services, a company under the Trathens umbrella, operated a short-lived tour of Richmond, and a service from central London to the Windsor Safari Park during the summers of 1984/85. Another associated company was Culturebus, which from May 1983 operated the first hop-on hop-off service, initially using five closed-top DMSs in a sprightly yellow livery.

One of the original quintet of 'Culturebuses' was DMS 1444 which was christened 'Nicholas Nickleby' and carried the number CB2. Culturebus was acquired by Ensign's in 1985 and this bus continued to work on the service for the new concern, suitably re-numbered to C207. Upon repaint it carried various advertisement liveries before it too passed to New Enterprise Coaches, where it held out until October 1990. G.A. Rixon

A bus which has never left the capital is DM 1078, having been a member of Len Wright's 'London Buslines' fleet for six years, before losing its roof and becoming one of the first Fleetlines to be operated by the Big Bus Company. It carried this advertising livery for a year before regaining fleet livery in July 1994, a month before it was caught crawling along Whitehall. G.A. Rixon

The maroon colours of the Big Bus Company first appeared on London's streets in June 1991 and they have since built up an impressive sightseeing fleet, mostly consisting of DMSs. Retaining its Leyland units, DMS 2326 is one of the many B20s owned which has been fully converted to open-top. It is seen in Whitehall in June 1994. G.A. Rixon

In the last months of 1985 the Ensign consortium purchased the competing operations of Culturebus and Ebdon's, and the vehicles of the London Tour Company (which had included DMS 1414) and London Cityrama were acquired in 1989 and 1993 respectively. London Pride has expanded as a result. It now operates not only a regular open-top stopping service, but also a new route connecting the Thames Barrier with central London, via the Woolwich Ferry and the new development in the Docklands area. London Pride continue to operate DMS 33, the earliest DMS in regular passenger service.

New companies continue to emerge, Blue Triangle and the Big Bus Company being recent additions, again mostly utilising Fleetlines in part or fully open-top form. London Sightseeing Tours were replaced by a new company called the London Hop-on Hop-off Service in 1993 and many of this fleet have had the entire centre doorway transplanted to the offside to ease loading on one-way streets, primarily at Haymarket. DMS 1935 additionally has a fixed canvas roof, a sensible compromise in view of the British climate, and it is a wonder other buses have not been similarly treated.

The blue liveried buses of London Cityrama ceased to operate at the end of 1993. DMS 2091 had been part of that fleet for over a decade, becoming a part open-topper in 1989. The Fleetlines of Cityrama were acquired by Ensign's and most were transferred to the associated London Pride Sightseeing, in whose fleet it is numbered 291. It normally operates on their new tourist service between Piccadilly and Greenwich, via the Woolwich Ferry and the Thames Barrier, where the bus is seen on a typically cloudy day in July 1994. N.J. Eadon-Clarke

DMS 2082 reached London Sightseeing Tours by way of Grimsby-Cleethorpes Transport and Enterprise & Silver Dawn. The offside door fitted to facilitate loading in one-way streets is clearly visible in this view at Marble Arch in 1994. N.J. Eadon-Clarke

London Buslines have been operating route 81 since 1985. DM 1078 was acquired at the outset and is picking up passengers at Hounslow West station two years later. This bus is now an open topper in the Sightseeing fleet of The Big Bus Company. N.J. Eadon-Clarke

LRT CONTRACT OPERATIONS

Since London Regional Transport began contracting routes in 1985, many Fleetlines have remained within the former central area boundary. The very first batch of tenders included route 81 (Hounslow–Slough), awarded to London Buslines from 13th July 1985 and operated by nine DMs acquired from Ensign. The buses initially proved unreliable, but undaunted they purchased a further six examples after gaining route 195 (Charville Lane Estate–Hanwell) from 12th April 1986. They have been gradually replaced by newer buses over the years.

Tour operator London Cityrama took over route 200 (Raynes Park–Streatham Hill) from 22nd March 1986. They placed 12 examples into service in their dark blue livery, mostly DMs, but surrendered the tender from 1st December 1988 due to their declining resources for its operation. Most were then used on route 196 (Norwood Junction–Kennington), replacing former South Yorkshire Fleetlines, until its loss from 28th October 1989.

Next came Sampsons Coaches, who ran route 217B (later 317) between Upshire and Enfield from 24th May 1986 until the contract was terminated due to maintenance difficulties on 1st July 1988, operating with seven DMs and a solitary DMS. Metrobus of Orpington took delivery of 13 DMSs in August 1986, smartly attired in their dark blue and deep yellow livery, for operation primarily on routes 61/361 (Bromley North–Green Street Green/Orpington), but also frequently on route 261 (Bromley Common–Lewisham).

Ensignbus won its first LRT contract from 21st June 1986 and went on to amass a whole network in the outskirts of east London. Naturally, Fleetlines from the dealing stock were used, predominantly DMs. As further contracts were won the number of Fleetlines operated passed the 40 mark, until withdrawals began in 1990. On 29th December 1990 the stage operations were acquired by the CNT Group, owners of Citybus, Hong Kong.

Sampson's Coaches were awarded the LRT contract of route 217B from 24th May 1986, for which eight Fleetlines were acquired. Many saw little service and proved most unreliable, eventually leading to the loss of the tender. One of the better vehicles, DM 1119, is seen in better days at Waltham Cross in August. Gerald Mead

DMS 1684 was a late addition to the large fleet of Ensignbus, having previously been a vehicle available for hire and filming from the stock of Ted Brakell. Emerging in Ensign fleet livery as number 234 in July 1988, it was to last just three years before transferring to nearby Blue Triangle, where it was converted to open-top format and used on their Sightseeing service in London. Barking's Gascoigne Estate is the setting for this view. Mike Harris

SALES FROM THE ENSIGN BUS COMPANY

In early 1979 the disposal of all standard Fleetlines was approved. London Transport began to dispose of the skeletal bodies which for years had been kept at the back of garages, the Wombwell Diesels company being the main recipient. For the others, the Ensign Bus Company agreed exclusive rights to purchase all the remaining vehicles as their certificates of fitness expired. The name of Ensign first appeared in June 1973, being an amalgamation of the Passenger Vehicle Sales companies which had made a name for themselves from 1963 by dealing with the sales of serviceable vehicles of the RT classes. By the mid 1980s they had become an empire, with associated companies covering vehicle sales, engineering, sightseeing tours and LRT contracts.

Fleetline disposals became a goldmine for Ensign — young modern buses which could be refurbished and snapped up by operators for further service at reasonable prices. Buyers were offered overhauled buses, most being converted to single-door configuration and repainted into a myriad colour schemes. Others were delivered in grey primer, some companies preferring to apply their own liveries. Sale prices varied, but averaged at about a seventh of the cost of a new double-decker.

The first DMSs were received in April 1979 and over the following 15 years nearly 1,800 examples passed through their books. A third of these saw no further use and were stripped of parts and subsequently scrapped. The remainder lived on. Over 330 examples were acquired by municipal operators and National Bus companies, and a further 80 were ordered by the West Midlands Passenger Transport Executive. Buying large capacity secondhand double-deckers had traditionally been forced upon only the smaller operators, and the remainder found uses within this group or were exported. Ensign's one workshop and yard was situated at Grays. The site quickly proved to be inadequate, resulting in much work being sub-contracted to small operators, who in some cases then took a vehicle in exchange for the work carried out. By the summer of 1981 a 16-acre site at Purfleet had been found, and all of the stock (numbering over a thousand vehicles, of which over 700 were Fleetlines) transferred to this location. Prior to this, buses had been stored in a disused area of the Royal Albert Docks.

After selection for refurbishment, each bus was cleaned inside and out and given a thorough mechanical overhaul, many major components being replaced by reconditioned units. Unusually, engines were derated in an attempt to prolong their lives. Whilst the buses were structurally sound, staff nevertheless checked the stress areas and replaced damaged panelling. Centre exits were removed at this stage; at first the Department of Transport advised that the doorway partitions should be retained to avoid structural weakness, but it was soon agreed that the removal of the bulkheads did not alter the overall body strength. Thus early Mark I conversions were fitted with a shortened side window and an inward facing bench seating three, whereas later examples (Mark IIs) received a standard window bay and conventional forward-facing seating. On all DMSs the Automatic Fare Collecting unit was removed, and replaced by a luggage pen or extra seating. Back-to-back seating could be applied over the rear wheelarches, and the single upstairs seat behind the staircase could be replaced by a double, thereby increasing capacities on dual-doored buses to between 71-75, and up to 79 on single-doored conversions.

Experiments by their engineers produced a few oddities. Early 1981 saw the appearance of DMS 729, rebuilt as a prototype left-hand drive demonstrator with offside dual-doors, incorporating twin headlamps and full-depth sliding windows. In 1983 they shortened the chassis of DM 1758 to just 23ft, and its body was

DMS 729, converted by Ensign into a left-hand drive export demonstrator after its success with the first sales of the type to Hong Kong. This vehicle was later exported to the USA. Malcolm King

DM 1758 was the subject of an apprentices' exercise at Ensign. The vehicle was never used in this form and saw out its days as a seat store at the company's Purfleet yard. N.J. Eadon-Clarke

suitably re-panelled to fit. This was part of a project for a short-wheelbased Fleetline, which came to nothing. Eight years later its remains were scrapped.

By far the most ambitious project was carried out on DMS 2148, completely rebuilt during early 1983. It emerged with an 'Ensign Enterprise' front, upper deck windscreen wipers, tinted windows and the new registration KJN7Y, unrecognisable as a DMS. It had coach seating for 62. DMS 590 followed suit in 1984 (re-registered A741TTW), and DMS 237 made a trio in 1985 (re-registered B56DAR). The latter two had a revised interior layout which catered for 65 passengers. All were purchased by Londoners Tacho Ltd, associated with The Londoners coach company, and used exclusively on contract work in central London. Only DMS 237 remains mobile, having been re-fitted as an optician's testing centre.

A fourth conversion, to a slightly different 'Ensign Executive' design, was completed on DMS 852 in 1985 (re-registered 31DOO). It had luxury seating for 31, with bar, reception desk and video. It was initially used as a hospitality unit by Ensign's themselves, before being sold to the brewers Guinness in 1988. Many received open-top conversions by Ensign's, and six have received an open rear balcony. Of these, DMSs 1469, 1943 and DM 1800 also received an 'Ensign Enterprise' front.

Three DMSs were converted into coach specification for The Londoners Tacho, Peckham. They were mainly employed on contracted Sightseeing work in London. The first two are seen here parked on the Embankment in 1985. Former DMS 2148 is behind DMS 590. N.J. Eadon-Clarke

Ensign converted DMS 852 into an Executive Hospitality Unit. Looking extremely smart, it is seen at their Purfleet premises in 1986.
N.J. Eadon-Clarke

In 1988 DMS 852 was sold to Arthur Guinness & Sons (GB) Ltd and was first used in support of their Saloon car racing sponsorship. It is seen here in use at Brands Hatch Racing Circuit.
N.J. Eadon-Clarke

The Yorkshire independent Woods of Mirfield operated DMS 769 for four years. It was unusual in having the name 'Fleetliner' added at the front and its towing panel has been replaced by what appears to be a Reliance grille. Upon sale, it spent a further two years with the Mansfield Coronets before departing for scrap. Mike Fowler

Midland Fox, and Midland Red (East) before them, have been great admirers of the Fleetline and have owned over 120 examples, which include B20s. Typical of the earliest batch delivered in early 1982 is DM 1769 (numbered 2769), which rallied on until being replaced in April 1990. It is seen in August 1982 in NBC poppy red livery. G.A. Rixon

OTHER OPERATORS

Sceptics in the seventies would not have believed that the class would remain in such strength into the nineties. Many vehicles have given sterling service to owners who took the chance to purchase in the early eighties and no fewer than 40 continue in use having been with sole owners for over 10 years. The longevity record belongs to DMS 1307, still going strong after 15 years as a mobile showroom with Ciba-Geigy, based at Duxford, this after only seven years of use by London Transport. Of those in service, DM 1181 has been a consistent performer with Hornsby Travel since September 1981.

The DMS attracted varied customers. One of the most enthusiastic was Midland Red (East), later to become Midland Fox, who have run up to 80 examples from 1982. Upon replacement in 1992, a batch of 28 B20s were purchased which now mix freely with the seven examples remaining of the standard type. Large quantities were also operated by Western National, Western Scottish and Wilts & Dorset, while a score of vehicles saw service with Grimsby-Cleethorpes, Greater Manchester PTE, Maidstone & District and Midland Red (North). Despite the various liveries carried, no DMS has yet appeared in the stripes of Stagecoach!

Apart from the Ensign group, the biggest independent operator has been Stevensons of Spath. DMS operation began in September 1979 and was to last for 13 years. During that time 70 of the class had been owned, although many did not operate, merely being acquired for vehicle parts or subsequent sale. Parts were required as the company was one of the pioneers of the single-door conversion and, apart from a few 1985 acquisitions, all of their fleet was treated.

In 1982 former DMS 1689 was rebuilt using parts from four other vehicles. Such was the amount of work involved the bus qualified for a 'new' registration and received CBF31Y. This view shows the rebuilt vehicle about to leave Uttoxeter bus station in 1986. This vehicle is still owned by Stevensons as a tree lopper. N.J. Eadon-Clarke

For the past five years DM 1121 and DMS 1538 have operated on the hop-on hop-off open-topped tour around the historic city of Bath, a service provided by Ryan's of Langridge. DMS 1304 has been roofless since 1980, and operates with the ever-expanding Guide Friday company, having spent the summer of 1994 traversing the delights of Brighton. Converted to open-top in 1990 following a low bridge accident, DMS 1491 has since then been used by Crosville Cymru on their summer coastal service between Rhyl and Llandudno.

When it was the turn of the B20s to be sold, many of these were also eagerly snapped up for further service. Midland Fox, G.K. Kinch, Bullocks of Cheadle, Mayne's of Manchester and Stuart Palmer Travel took quantities. Unfortunately, half of the B20 fleet was scrapped, despite the fitting of Iveco engines to many. Perhaps it is easy to forget that these buses were 15 years old at this time and that their life expectancy had been achieved.

Only a few Fleetlines have carried cherished registrations within the UK. One of the first was the placing of DDA66 onto DMS 1893. Between 1985-90 DMS 1981 carried the prestigious 1NTG, initials of its owner North Thames Gas; it has since been re-registered MMK668P. GVV205 was carried on London Pride's DMS 353 during 1990, and Hutchison Telecommunications DMS 1967 was given HTL446 in 1992. The Routemaster mark WLT916 was placed upon D 2633 by LBL; just prior to its sale it was further changed to DGJ415S. The ages of Bennett's Coaches DM 1086 and DMS 1619 were hidden in 1994 when they received the Irish registrations RJI 5702/1 respectively.

The unusual livery of Beestons is typified here by former DMS 2212 which stands at Long Melford station yard. N.J. Eadon-Clarke

In 1993 Bennetts of Chieveley acquired a second DMS for school contracts and both were subsequently re-registered. The original DMS 1619 (RJI5701) formerly with Windsorian stands next to DM 1086 (RJI5702) which had previously operated for Alpha Coaches of Hull. Bennett's yard is the location of this May 1994 view. N.J. Eadon-Clarke

Haven Bus, Newhaven are now owned by Blue Triangle. They run several standard DMSs and also B20 types. The fleet is now receiving the livery of the parent company as evidenced by DMS 2314 seen opposite the Palace Pier, Brighton in August 1994. N.J. Eadon-Clarke

R. Bullock of Cheadle have an operational fleet of five DMSs, four of which are B20 types. The exception is former DM 1216 picking up passengers at Manchester's Arndale centre. This vehicle was acquired from Grimsby-Cleethorpes. N.J. Eadon-Clarke

The side advertisement on former DMS 2321 spoils the smart livery of Busybus of Boxmoor. Here it stands at Radlett on its regular working, schooldays route 861, under contract to Hertfordshire County Council. N.J. Eadon-Clarke

A very smart DM 1002 stands in the yard of its owner J.H. Pollard & Son, trading as Cherry Tree Coaches, at The Lizard. It has been owned for over twelve years and is used mostly for school contracts. N.J. Eadon-Clarke

Chesterfield Transport took delivery of its first DMSs in February 1980 and was quickly to amass a mixed fleet of 16, an equal share of Park Royal and MCW examples. One of the latter was DMS 1415 which became their number 162, and which gave the municipality nine years service before withdrawal. Mike Fowler

DMS 656 operated for Viceroy Coaches of Saffron Walden for seven years in a patchwork orange livery of its previous owner Graham's of Paisley. It passed to Connor & Graham in 1992 and again operated initially in that livery. In spring 1994 it received the very smart C&G livery a few months before the company sold out to East Yorkshire. N.J. Eadon-Clarke

DM 1827 operated with Cedar Coaches of Bedford for seven years before it was re-sold to Crosskeys Tours of Newingreen. It stands outside Hythe swimming pool awaiting school children on 5th July 1993. N.J. Eadon-Clarke

Originally a 1980 Ensign's single-door conversion for Western National, DMS 1491 has since had a varied career, having reached Crosville Cymru in 1990 after passing through various coach companies at Clayworth and Speke. Not long after being numbered HDL921, it received roof damage and was converted to open-top. For the past five summers it has been employed on Crosville's 'Happy Dragon' open-top service along the North Wales coast. Mike Harris

Initially DMS 1283 was the only MCW bodied example acquired by Derby City Transport. Three more were obtained from Thamesdown in 1986 in exchange for Dominators. DMS 1283 is seen sporting a new 'Roe' style front dome in 1985, following roof damage. N.J. Eadon-Clarke

M.J. de Courcey own a DM, a DMS and a part open-top South Yorkshire PTE example. DMS 2129 is in the Coventry depot yard. N.J. Eadon-Clarke

One of the last DMs to be delivered in 1978, DM 2634 was first allocated to Stockwell garage for use primarily on route 168, but it often appeared also on the Round London Sightseeing Tour. Converted into a D in early 1981, its life was prolonged by the fitment of an Iveco engine in 1989. It now operates for Filer's of Ilfracombe, in whose garage yard it is seen.
N.J. Eadon-Clarke

Former DMS 652 had been used as a demonstrator by Ensign before being purchased by Graham's of Paisley. Mr Finch of Wigan visited Graham's to buy a surplus DMS, but didn't like that being offered and after further negotiation he obtained this bus, seen in April 1989, which Graham's had been reluctant to part with.
N.J. Eadon-Clarke

DMS 1968 was the only MCW bodied DMS to be fitted from new with a Rolls-Royce Eagle engine. It ran with this engine for many years with David Grasby, often requiring the fitting of hand built parts. It stands at the Oxhill base five days after repainting into this unusual livery in 1988 which it still carries.
N.J. Eadon-Clarke

The bus displays destination **AWKHEAD** with fleet number **D30** and registration **OJD 129R**. Advertisement reads SHARP CALCULATORS with the equation $a^2 = b^2 + c^2 - 2bc \cos A$. Fleet name **GRAHAM'S BUS SERVICE LTD**.

The once-famous Graham's Bus Services of Paisley operated a fleet of 20 DM/Ss, of which DMS 2129 was a single-doored delivery of 1982. All received this distinctive livery, shown in Seedhill Road during 1984. The bus passed to Mike de Courcey Travel of Coventry in 1988, where it continues in use (see page 50). N.J. Eadon-Clarke

Facing Page Upper **Hornsby Travel added one B20 type D to their existing stock. D 2542 stands at their Ashby base with DM 1137 behind, the latter withdrawn in August 1994 after fire damage.** N.J. Eadon-Clarke

Facing Page Lower **Horsham Coaches have owned several DMSs over the years; their current example is DM 1029 which reached Horsham after spells with Southend Transport and Black Horse, Gravesend. It stands at Warnham station in summer 1994.** N.J. Eadon-Clarke

DM 1020 has had a multitude of owners. It first operated on London Sightseeing with Ebdons before being re-acquired by Ensign where it joined their bus fleet. It then passed to Haven Coaches before being sold to J&J Coachlines in whose Kent yard it is seen in June 1994 in their unusual livery. This vehicle has been retrimmed internally with a very smart maroon moquette. N.J. Eadon-Clarke

G.K. Kinch acquired a quantity of B20 type DMSs to operate their Nottingham route 48 and new services in Leicester. Former DMS 2340 is seen in Nottingham in late 1992. Route 48 is now operated by former London Leyland Titans. N.J. Eadon-Clarke

Maidstone & District acquired twenty DMSs for service. One of the original vehicles was DMS 2069 standing on the exit ramp of The Pentagon shopping centre in Chatham. On withdrawal it passed to the New Enterprise subsidiary and is now owned by Green Lane Travel of Muswell Hill. N.J. Eadon-Clarke

DMS 1451 is an example of an early single-door conversion by Ensign. The interior bulkheads were retained and an inward facing bench seat was fitted. It is seen at Ballieston with Marshall's who retained the livery of its former owner (Graham's of Paisley). N.J. Eadon-Clarke

Mybus of Hadfield ran a fleet of B20 DMSs in Manchester. A broad cream band was added to the LT red. DMS 2497 is seen at Manchester Piccadilly in May 1993. After cessation of services, their fleet of B20s was exported to Hong Kong. Mike Harris

The oldest DMS operated by Maidstone & District was 1658. It has now passed to subsidiary company New Enterprise of Tonbridge where it is seen in June 1994. N.J. Eadon-Clarke

City of Oxford was another early customer for DMSs. One of the first was DMS 1274 seen in Oxford in 'Park & Ride' livery in 1985. N.J. Eadon-Clarke

Stuart Palmer of Dunstable took the opportunity to acquire over a dozen B20 type DMSs for use on local services and school contracts. The fleet is represented here by former DMS 2481. N.J. Eadon-Clarke

Red Rover of Aylesbury obtained two DMSs in 1979. Former DMS 437 demonstrates their original livery in Aylesbury town centre in 1980. N.J. Eadon-Clarke

Premier Travel of Cambridge obtained five DMSs in 1985 and further examples with the take-over of Youngs of Rampton. On withdrawal in 1988 one of the original buses, DMS 1989, passed to the dealer Claireaux of Hadleigh. After a period with Partridge Coaches, it passed to Red & Green of Chislehurst where it has proved a very reliable vehicle. It stands at Dartford Heath.
N.J. Eadon-Clarke

DMS 1538 is one of two ex-London Fleetlines used by Ryan's of Langridge on sightseeing work in Bath.
N.J. Eadon-Clarke

The first DMS to be re-registered in the UK was DMS 1893 by Shorey of Maulden. It stands with three other DMSs in the operator's yard carrying its new number DDA66 and original livery in 1987. N.J. Eadon-Clarke

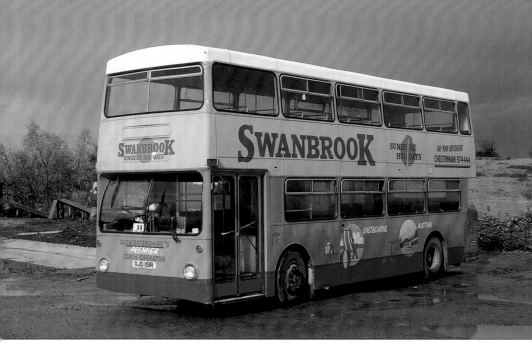

Former DMS 2151 was the last DMS to operate with Stevensons. It then passed to Swanbrook in whose yard it poses for the camera. N.J. Eadon-Clarke

Venture Travel of Cardiff operated former DM 995 in LT livery for many years. In autumn 1993 it finally received fleet livery as seen in this view taken in their yard just after painting. An LT side blind is still fitted. N.J. Eadon-Clarke

Seen passing through picturesque Hampton Court is Wealden of London's number 51, formerly DMS 849. It is operating on their shortlived 'Richmond Heritage Ride' during the summer of 1984. Upon sale the bus was to see a further three years service with the North Wales independent Gold Star. G.A. Rixon

Western Scottish obtained 32 DMSs between 1982 and 1984. When the company was split some passed to the new Clydeside company and some of these were destined to return to London for Bexleybus. Former DMS 1986 represents one of those that remained with Western Scottish and stands in Kilmarnock bus station on a wet day in 1990 in the final livery style. N.J. Eadon-Clarke

One of a number of DMSs obtained for playbus conversion is 808, now the 'Banbury & District Community Bus'. It poses for the camera at its home base in Steeple Aston. N.J. Eadon-Clarke

NON-PSV CUSTOMERS

As well as PSV work, DMSs have proved most capable of being rebuilt or adapted for a range of uses, in either mobile or static mode. The most common have been as film catering, exhibition or hospitality units, advertising or publicity vehicles, and of course playbuses, where their spacious interiors can be utilised to the full. They have proved most popular with bands and touring groups where the performers can sit upstairs whilst their mass of equipment is packed downstairs. More extreme have been singular conversions into a fashion shop, a community centre, an optician's, a library and a health clinic.

A few have made the journey across the Channel and can be seen in Belgium, France, Germany, Italy and Spain. The DMS also flies the British flag further worldwide, although none have yet ventured into Australasia. Vehicles have been reported in Canada, Finland, Turkey and on St Lucia, part of the Windward Islands. Recent exports have seen examples appear in Nigeria and other parts of Africa.

Many have already been earmarked for future preservation, but so far only four can be truly termed preserved. DMS 1 is part of the London Transport Museum Collection, whilst DMS 2246 is a static exhibit in a French museum. The Leyland engined prototype DMS 132 is under restoration into original 1971 condition, whilst DMS 2456 has been repainted all red, a reminder of its return in 1985 from Ogle Designs at Letchworth where it was upgraded with the recommendations which led up to the modern day DiPTAC conversions. It has a unique seating layout of H41/23D following the installation of a forward facing staircase directly behind the driver.

Basildon Council acquired DMS 841 for use as a playbus in 1987. It is seen in Basildon in 1990. This vehicle is now a playbus with Thurrock Council, but still carries signwriting for Basil Badger. N.J. Eadon-Clarke

The BBC World Service use former DMS 25 to promote their service throughout Europe. It has travelled as far afield as Russia. A former open-top sightseeing bus, it has a canvas roof so that it can pass under the European 4 metre high bridges. On arrival the roof is raised on telescopic poles. It poses for the camera in summer 1994 in Ensign's yard. N.J. Eadon-Clarke

After use by Brighton Transport the Leyland-engined prototype DMS 132 was sold to Whitbread Inns for use as a playbus. It is seen in Lingfield in October 1993. This bus has now been acquired for preservation. N.J. Eadon-Clarke

The Bus Cafe, former DM 982, is seen in active use at Penblwyn roundabout near Narberth on the A40. The upper deck was used as living accommodation while the lower deck contained wooden tables and chairs. The kitchen was a separate trailer parked behind with access to the bus through the lower deck emergency exit. The bus wore the livery of its former owner Capitol of Cwmbran and was scrapped in 1992. N.J. Eadon-Clarke

Charly Records are reputed to have spent £75,000 fitting out this vehicle with CD and Video equipment. The former DMS 806 stands out of use at their warehouse and is currently for sale.
N.J. Eadon-Clarke

DM 1031 operated for many years in LT red for Swaffham Coachways before receiving their blue/yellow livery in 1987. After withdrawal in 1989 it became the Downham Market Area Community Playbus, where it is seen in September 1991.
N.J. Eadon-Clarke

The Dyfed Fire and Rescue Service, Carmarthen, own DMS 136 which is used at schools and local events to educate children about the dangers of fire. It is parked at the Dyfed Fire Service headquarters and is highly regarded as a means of getting the message across.
N.J. Eadon-Clarke

Former DM 1160 was converted for the Dyfed Wildlife Trust based at Cardigan Bay with assistance from 'The Help Squad', an ITV programme. It was one of the four ex-Bexleybus vehicles to be repainted with a red front, which it retains with the Trust. N.J. Eadon-Clarke

DMS 2206 was lucky to survive an engine fire during delivery to Hants & Dorset. It returned to Ensign, and after conversion and use by Spafax it was bought by Falcon Cycles of Brigg as a mobile bicycle showroom. Maintenance was contracted to Moodies at Liphook in whose yard it is parked in 1989. N.J. Eadon-Clarke

General Foods Ltd, Banbury, operate former DMS 294 as a mobile 'Roadshow' for their products. It carries an appropriate registration 'JGF' since it is driven by 'John' for 'General Foods'. In this view it is in use in Regents Park in August 1988. The addition of a front grille enhances an otherwise drab front. N.J. Eadon-Clarke

In 1994 Arthur Guinness & Sons repainted their Hospitality Bus, former DMS 852, into 'Guinness' colours to recognise the achievement of the Irish Football Team reaching the World Cup Finals. It poses for the camera in Ensign's yard at Rainham in July 1994. N.J. Eadon-Clarke

Now in its twelfth year with the Harlow Council for Voluntary Service, DMS 276 continues in its use as a playbus. Pictured in its original livery in May 1986, it was repainted into an allover dark blue livery in the summer of 1993 and has yet to have its additional rainbow stripes applied. Gerald Mead

An early sale for non-PSV use in 1982 was DMS 1449 which is used as transport by the Harlow Majorettes. It is parked at Thornwood Common in July 1993. N.J. Eadon-Clarke

Viceroy Coaches of Saffron Walden operated DM 1818 in LT red for some seven years. It was re-acquired by Ensign and sold to Anthony Briscoe Opticians in 1992. It was converted into a mobile opticians and used at USAF bases in Suffolk. This vehicle has now returned to Ensign and is again for sale. N.J. Eadon-Clarke

One of only half-a-dozen examples to be supplied by Ensign's with an open rear platform, DMS 2023 was also fitted out on both decks with a carpet for its intended use as a mobile conference and publicity bus. It was acquired by the Labour Party in 1984 and was used for nine years on political campaigns throughout the country. This livery was carried until 1988, when a second 'red rose' version was applied. The bus is currently in store with a London operator pending a decision upon its future. Malcolm King

The British Schools Technology establishment at Bedford converted DMS 2238 into an information technology bus in 1985. It was heralded as 'London's Open College Technobus'. Since then the bus has hardly been seen, but it was captured in November 1993 at New Cross whilst touring schools within the London Borough of Lewisham. Peter Bates

Former DMS 1515 was the subject of a unique conversion in 1991. The front third was retained, and mounted on the chassis behind it was a mock-up of part of a tube train and a part of a British Rail train. It was named Supercar and promoted the one day Travelcard in TV adverts and various events. Here it is at Southend shortly after conversion. N.J. Eadon-Clarke

DMS 358 has been owned by the Lowestoft Playbus Association for almost ten years. It is seen in active use at the Norfolk Showground in August 1994. N.J. Eadon-Clarke

A unique use for a DMS was as this bridge maintenance unit, a joint venture between Maidstone & District and Network SouthEast. Former DM 1090 is on display at the St Albans rally in 1990. N.J. Eadon-Clarke

North Thames Gas ran this mobile exhibition bus to demonstrate gas fires. Here DMS 1981 with cherished registration is on display at Great Mills superstore, Ashford. The vehicle was later exported to Turkey. N.J. Eadon-Clarke

Ensign converted two vehicles for Philips. In 1987, DMS 1943 operated on its own, but from 1988 it was joined by DM 1800. Here the former is seen arriving on Brighton seafront in summer 1989. The sliding roof can be clearly seen. N.J. Eadon-Clarke

The Post Office use two DMSs to tour schools. One is DMS 1988, the 'Write it' bus which attempts to encourage children to write letters and is seen in the Kidbrooke engineering yard. N.J. Eadon-Clarke

The other vehicle is DMS 2005 seen in the Kidbrooke engineering yard fresh out of the paint shop in October 1990. N.J. Eadon-Clarke

Project Otter was designed to give schoolchildren an insight into the environment of the Otter. DMS 1942 was fitted out with various audio visual displays. It resides at Old Holt Farm, Edingworth. N.J. Eadon-Clarke

DM 1212 is an exhibition unit for Royal Mail. It had previously been an exhibition unit with 3M (UK) and Jeffcock Security. N.J. Eadon-Clarke

The Stirling Superbus, former DMS 290, is seen in playbus use in Bannockburn in 1990 in its stunning livery. The vehicle was formerly a mobile creche with the London Borough of Islington. N.J. Eadon-Clarke

Surrey Heath Leisure Services acquired DMS 1850 in 1988 and converted it into a playbus named 'Monty'. It had spent the previous three years with the South Oxfordshire Technical College.

DMS 2155 is now 12-1376 with the Guangzhou Number One Bus Company. It also has a new roof having been open-top with its former owner, Citybus, Hong Kong. N.J. Eadon-Clarke

OVERSEAS SALES

By far the best customers for the type have been operators in Hong Kong. The China Motor Bus Company received 206 examples, whilst the Kowloon Motor Bus Company took delivery of 100; a further 59 were shared between the Argos Bus Company and Citybus. All were prepared for export by Ensign.

The order for China Motor Bus was sub-contracted from London Transport. All were re-fitted with full-depth sliding windows, fareboxes and H44/27D seating (although licensed for H44/29D with 26 standees). DMS 438 alone was more extensively rebuilt; it was first displayed at the 1980 Cobham bus rally where it was exhibited with a half-width front door, the remainder of the entrance being incorporated into the bodywork increasing the seating to H44/32D. At least 73 remained in use during the summer of 1994, some in their 14th year on the Island.

The Hong Kong buses operated in grossly overcrowded conditions, often in 90-degree humidity on high intensity 20-hour congested routes. In this arduous environment they worked extremely well, a compliment not normally directed to the type! Over 40 have been purchased by Speedybus Services Ltd; most are time expired vehicles from Kowloon and Citybus, but recent purchases of B20s have been made from dealers in South Yorkshire. Most have been fitted with additional offside double-doors and leased for further service within the People's Republic of China. All have all-over advertising liveries, mostly for cigarette brands.

More unusual were the three DMSs bought by Chung Wah Shipbuilding for staff transport. Ensign had removed the central exit and rear half of the entrance doorway, leaving just a 2ft wide access. Three-by-two seating was installed on both decks, with a backwards facing bench seat at the front upstairs, back-to-back seats over the rear wheels, and a forward facing seat for three adjacent to the driver. They entered service in 1981, having been reduced in seating upon export from an incredible 115 to just 102 (as H59/43F!) when the Hong Kong government refused to sanction the use of tip-up isle seat extensions

The panelled over doors can be seen in this view of former DMS 2165 outside Canton Railway Station in 1994 while operating for the Guangzhou company. N.J. Eadon-Clarke

DM 1227 was purchased by the Hong Kong Red Cross in 1983, and was converted into a blood donation/collection centre for the Hong Kong Blood Transfusion Service by Transport Supplies Worldwide, a dealer on the island. It is maintained by the engineers of Citybus, who numbered it D 47 within their fleet for ease of recording. It has never been issued with a Hong Kong registration, operating on trade plates. It is seen at work in May 1993, and it continues to serve the community. N.J. Eadon-Clarke

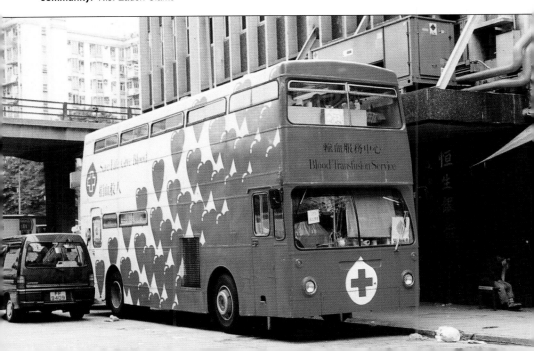

DMS 1691 has been a stalwart of sightseeing tours since 1984, having operated in open-top form for both Ensign's and London Sightseeing Tours before being shipped to New York in early 1993. It appeared for Apple Tours in a revised maroon/red livery for the 1994 season (having had the compulsory offside doors fitted), as shown when pictured at Batten Park. Mike Fowler

Facing Page Upper **One of the first buses to operate for Apple Tours of New York was DM 1093 in 1992. Formerly a closed top example in the fleet of London Sightseeing Tours, it was converted to open-top and fitted with offside doors. By 1994 it had been decorated in advertisement livery, as depicted in the locality of Greenwich Village. Numbered 12 in their fleet, it carries its second New York registration number.** Mike Fowler

Facing Page Lower **DMS 1414 was initially used by Ensign as a demonstrator before passing to Arrow Travel and then to London Sightseeing duties. It stands in Chicago with Chicago Motor Coach offering 'Polite Transportation' with its centre exit doors intact, making alighting and boarding somewhat hazardous in American streets.** N.J. Eadon-Clarke

Customs officials of the United States of America have accepted 61 imports, of which 38 currently operate on tours of Chicago and New York, with examples soon to appear on the streets of Washington. Six closed top DMSs in a colourful union jack livery continue to operate contracts in and around the mountains at Denver.

Nearer home, but nevertheless over the water in Ireland, DMS 1838 operates on the Gray Line Tour of Dublin, re-registered 7997ZW, whilst in France DMS 1485 is used for hospitality uses, which include tours, by Publibus.

Chicago Motor Coach have been using DMSs on sightseeing tours since 1986. This view of 559 (DMS 586) was taken at Chicago Water Tower in summer 1992. The vehicle has gained an offside door, but carries the livery of its former owner, London Pride Sightseeing. It did not operate with this livery in London. N.J. Eadon-Clarke

The DMSs with New York Apple Tours that retain their roofs for operation during the winter have clear perspex centre roof panels to allow tourists to look up at tall buildings. This view shows this feature inside DM 1015. N.J. Eadon-Clarke

APPENDIX ONE The Survivors

This list gives details of the ownership of ex-London Transport D/DM/DMS family vehicles (totalling 765) at the time of privatisation of London Buses Ltd (September/October 1994). Any vehicles illustrated in the main part of the book and not listed here had been scrapped.

1	London Transport Collection, Covent Garden Museum	H44/24D	Preserved
6	Trathens Restaurant Complex, Orange, France	H/D	static cafeteria
25	BBC World Service, West Acton	O/D	Exhibition Unit
33	London Pride Sightseeing, Rainham [333]	O45/23F	
36	Film Wheels Ltd, Denham	H/C	Film Catering Unit
39	Wokingham Playbus Association, Wokingham	H/D	Playbus
102	Fare Catering & Marquee Ltd, Chiddingfold	H/F	Hospitality Unit
104	Apple Tours, New York [37]	O45/23F	un-registered 1994
106	Argos Bus Services, Tsing Yi, Hong Kong [23]	H59/31D	re-reg DC 4129 1984
115	Oxford Playbus Association, Cowley	H/D	Playbus
132	Mr P Simmonds, Morden	H44/24D	Preserved
136	Dyfed Fire & Rescue Service, Carmarthen	H/D	Exhibition Unit
141	Apple Tours, New York, USA [14]	O44/26F*	re-reg BD 5337 1993 season, re-reg BD 5324 1994 season, further re-reg BE 4081 1994
142	Guangzhou No 1 Bus Company, Canton, China [1388]	H45/28F*	re-reg DC 5878 1984, re-reg 01-33452 1992
147	British Double Deckers, Denver, USA [BDD001]	H44/24D	re-reg AGY 927 1984; named "Paddington"
153	Guangzhou No 1 Bus Company, Canton, China [1389]	H45/28F*	re-reg DE 2138 1985, re-reg 01-33451 1992
158	London Pride Sightseeing, Rainham [358]	O45/23D	
165	London Pride Sightseeing, Rainham [365]	O45/23F	
167	China Motor Bus, North Point, Hong Kong [XF71]	H44/27D	re-reg CM 2483 1981
178	Autopilot Power Props Ltd, Greenwich	H/D	Film Promotion Unit
180	British Double Deckers, Denver, USA [BDD002]	H44/24D	re-reg AGY 930 1984; named "Camelot"
185	British Double Deckers, Denver, USA [BDD003]	H44/24D	re-reg AGY 924 1984; named "Trafalgar"
188	London Pride Sightseeing, Rainham [388]	O45/23D	
191	Isle of Sheppey Playbus Association, Sheerness	H/D	Playbus
192	Double Deck Coach Tours, Chicago, USA [558]	O45/28C*	re-reg 19798 H from 1992
200	Savoir Fare & Party Rentals, Nuneaton	H/D	Hospitality Unit
211	British Double Deckers, Denver, USA [BDD004]	H44/24D	re-reg AGY 931 1984; named "Liverpool"; withdrawn 1994
227	Basingstoke Council for Community Service, Tadley	H/D	Coffee Shop
232	British Double Deckers, Denver, USA [BDD005]	H44/24D	re-reg AGY 928 1984, and AHE 1798 1994; named "Chelsea"
237	Templeman Opticians Ltd, Shoeburyness	H/C	re-reg B56 DAR 1985 following rebuild; Opticians Test Centre
255	London Pride Sightseeing, Rainham [355]	O45/27D	
259	Unknown group, Birmingham	H/D	Playbus
270	Unknown owner(s), Africa	H/C	former Playbus
276	Harlow Council for Voluntary Service, Harlow	H/C	Playbus
279	London Pride Sightseeing, Rainham [309]	O45/23D	
283	British Double Deckers, Denver, USA [BDD006]	H44/24D	re-reg AGY 925 1994; named "Picadilly" (sic)
287	London Pride Sightseeing, Rainham [387]	O45/23F	
290	Stirling District Council, Stirling	H/D	Creche - "Stirling Superbus"
294	General Foods Ltd, Banbury	H/F	Hospitality Unit - "Food Service Road Show"
299	Posh Nosh Ltd, Towcester	H/D	Restaurant
301	Argos Bus Services, Tsing Yi, Hong Kong [24]	H59/31D	re-reg DC 5287 1984
304	British Double Deckers, Denver, USA [BDD007]	H44/24D	re-reg AGY 929 1994; named "Baker St"
312	British Double Deckers, Denver, USA [BDD010]	H44/24D	used for spares since 1984
315	London Pride Sightseeing, Rainham [315]	O45/23D	
316	China Motor Bus, North Point, Hong Kong [XF44]	H44/27D	re-reg CG 8327 1980
322	London Pride Sightseeing, Rainham [322]	O45/27D	
326	Pleasurewood Hills American Theme Park, Corton	H44/31F	Courtesy Bus
329	Savoir Fare & Party Rentals, Nuneaton	H/D	Hospitality Unit

335	Argos Bus Services, Tsing Yi, Hong Kong [22]	H59/31D	re-reg DC 3484 1984
340	British Double Deckers, Denver, USA [BDD009]	H44/24D	re-reg AGY 926 1984
343	Stars P.V.B.A., Belgium	O45/23D	Promotional Unit
347	London Hop-on Hop-off Service, Bermondsey	O44/26F*	
358	Lowestoft Playbus Association, Lowestoft	H/D	Playbus
363	British Double Deckers, Denver, USA [BDD008]	H44/24D	re-reg AHP 183 1984; named "Big Ben"
370	China Motor Bus, North Point, Hong Kong [XF45]	H44/27D	re-reg CH 2961 1980
372	Apple Tours, New York, USA [28]	O44/26F*	re-reg BD 5309 1994 season, further re-reg BD 5303 1994
374	China Motor Bus, North Point, Hong Kong [XF26]	H44/27D	re-reg CF 2681 1980
402	Livingston Dining Services Ltd, Shepperton	H/D	Film Catering Unit
404	Blue Triangle Buses, Rainham [DMS404]	O44/25D	
406	Argos Bus Services, Tsing Yi, Hong Kong [26]	H59/31D	re-reg DC 5896 1984
408	Livingston Dining Services Ltd, Shepperton	H/D	Film Catering Unit
410	Farleigh Coaches, Wouldham	H44/29F	
413	China Motor Bus, North Point, Hong Kong [XF42]	H44/27D	re-reg CG 5287 1980
414	China Motor Bus, North Point, Hong Kong [XF43]	H44/27D	re-reg CG 8084 1980
416	Struan Motors Ltd, Perth	H/C	Publicity Unit
418	unknown owner(s), Finland	H44/27F	
420	China Motor Bus, North Point, Hong Kong [XF36]	H44/27D	re-reg CG 1496 1980
426	China Motor Bus, North Point, Hong Kong [XF19]	H44/27D	re-reg CE 5261 1980
428	Ringwood Public Address Systems Ltd, Ringwood	H/F	Showroom
438	China Motor Bus, North Point, Hong Kong [XF34]	H44/32D	re-reg CG 1081 1980
479	China Motor Bus, North Point, Hong Kong [XF58]	H44/27D	re-reg CJ 7614 1980
480	China Motor Bus, North Point, Hong Kong [XF22]	H44/27D	re-reg CE 6250 1980
482	China Motor Bus, North Point, Hong Kong [XF24]	H44/27D	re-reg CE 8626 1980
550	Kent Auto Auctions Ltd, Canterbury (dealer)	H/C	for sale since 1993, former Design & Technology Unit
553	Wacton Trading, Bromyard (dealer)	H/D	for sale since 1993, former Film Catering Unit
557	China Motor Bus, North Point, Hong Kong [T19]	H44/24D	re-reg CW 7787 1982; Driver Trainer since 1982
582	Hadleigh Marching Militaire, Hadleigh	H44/0D	Lower deck used for carrying equipment
586	Double Deck Coach Tours, Chicago, USA [559]	O45/28C*	re-reg 19797 H from 1992
590	Mercury Passenger Services, Kingsnorth	CH43/22C	re-reg A741 TTW 1984 following rebuild; stored since 1989
605	Speedybus Services, Kowloon, Hong Kong	H44/27D	re-reg CY 8605 1983; storeroom since 1990
606	Argos Bus Services, Tsing Yi, Hong Kong [2]	H59/37F	re-reg CL 8005 1981
609	China Motor Bus, North Point, Hong Kong [XF57]	H44/27D	re-reg CJ 6798 1980
617	China Motor Bus, North Point, Hong Kong [XF53]	H44/27D	re-reg CJ 5597 1980
620	Lambeth Community Youth Steel Orchestra, Croydon	H45/0D	Lower deck used for carrying equipment
626	Argos Bus Services, Tsing Yi, Hong Kong [1]	H59/37F	re-reg CL 4086 1981
643	London Hop-on Hop-off Service, Bermondsey	O44/29F	
648	Screen Facilities Ltd, Stoke Prior	H/D	Film Catering Unit
652	F E Finch Bus & Coach Hire, Higher Ince	H44/32F	Gardner engine fitted 1992
656	East Yorkshire Motor Services, Kingston-upon-Hull [894]	H44/31F	
659	China Motor Bus, North Point, Hong Kong [XF49]	H44/27D	re-reg CJ 790 1980
660	China Motor Bus, North Point, Hong Kong [XF56]	H44/27D	re-reg CJ 5686 1980
663	Argos Bus Services, Tsing Yi, Hong Kong [3]	H59/37F	re-reg CM 3247 1981
664	Brandon's of Blackmore End, near Braintree	H44/24D	Used for spares since 1993
665	Geoff Ripley, Carlton (dealer)	H44/27F	for sale since 1993
668	Blue Triangle Buses, Rainham [DMS668]	H44/27F	
677	Brandon's of Blackmore End, near Braintree	H44/24D	
681	Leaside Buses - Stamford Hill [DMS681]	H44/24D	
685	Guangzhou No 1 Bus Company, Canton, China	H45/28F*	re-reg CM 4087 1981, re-reg 01-11??? 1988
698	Guangzhou No 1 Bus Company, Canton, China	H45/28F*	re-reg CM 4782 1981, re-reg 01-11??? 1988
700	unknown owner, Dali, China	H45/28F*	re-reg CN 3966 1981, re-reg 01-????? 1988
704	Castle Point Bus Company, Hadleigh	H44/32D	

707	Midland Fox, Leicester [2700]	H44/29F	
713	London Pride Sightseeing, Rainham [313]	O45/24D	
717	Apple Tours, New York, USA [6]	O44/26F*	re-reg BD 5305 1993 season, re-reg BD 5300 1994 season
719	Apple Tours, New York, USA [17]	O44/26F*	re-reg BD 5325 1993 season, re-reg BD 5305 1994 season, further re-reg BD 5337 1994
725	Guangzhou No 1 Bus Company, Canton, China	H45/28F*	re-reg CM 2856 1981, re-reg 01-11??? 1988
729	Double Deck Coach Tours, Chicago, USA [513]	O45/29D*	Left hand drive conversion 1981; re-reg 29238 H from 1986;used for spares from 1992
739	Guangzhou No 1 Bus Company, Canton, China	H45/28F*	re-reg CM 2857 1981, re-reg 01-11??? 1988
740	unknown owner, Tianjin, China	H45/28F*	re-reg CZ 5930 1983, re-reg 01-????? 1988
750	Argos Bus Services, Tsing Yi, Hong Kong [6]	H59/37F	re-reg CS 8179 1981
751	unknown owner, Fuzhou, China	H45/28F*	re-reg CM 8751 1981, re-reg 01-????? 1988
755	Dawlish Coaches, Dawlish	H44/28D	
758	unknown owner, Wuzhou, China	H45/28F*	re-reg CM 4841 1981, re-reg 01-????? 1988
759	Voel Coaches, Dyserth	H44/28D	
768	Blue Triangle Buses, Rainham [DMS768]	H44/24D	
784	unknown owner, Wuzhou, China	H45/28F*	re-reg CY 8517 1983, re-reg 01-????? 1988
785	Guangzhou No 1 Bus Company, Canton, China	H45/28F*	re-reg CY 4971 1983, re-reg 01-11??? 1988
789	Guangzhou No 1 Bus Company, Canton, China [1357]	H45/28F*	re-reg CN 2102 1981, re-reg 01-32070 1991
794	Kowloon Motor Bus Co., Kowloon, Hong Kong [2D101]	H44/27D	re-reg CV 9753 1982; Driver Trainer since 1986
796	Guangzhou No 1 Bus Company, Canton, China [1365]	H45/28F*	re-reg CP 2073 1981, re-reg 01-32074 1991
798	Argos Bus Services, Tsing Yi, Hong Kong [69]	H59/41F	re-reg CN 3376 1981
806	Charly Records Ltd, South Bermondsey	H/D	Hospitality Unit/Warehouse; for sale, stored since 1992
808	The Children's Society, Banbury	H/D	Playbus - "Banbury & District Community Bus"
813	Double Deck Coach Tours, Chicago, USA [557]	O45/28C*	re-reg 19796 H from 1992
816	London Pride Sightseeing, Rainham [316]	O45/27D	
820	Castle Point Bus Company, Hadleigh	H45/28D	used for spares since 1992
831	Wacton Trading, Bromyard (dealer)	H44/29F	for sale 1994; former transport for farm workers
832	China Motor Bus, North Point, Hong Kong [XF90]	H44/27D	re-reg CS 4823 1981
840	London Pride Sightseeing, Rainham [340]	O45/27F	
841	Thurrock Borough Council, Thurrock [TB2191]	H/D	Playbus - "Basil Badger's Toytown Bus"
852	Arthur Guinness & Sons (GB) Ltd, Park Royal	CH20/11C	re-reg 31 DOO 1985 following rebuild; Hospitality Unit
855	Roundabout Community Trust, Lowestoft	H/D	Playbus - "The Magic Bus"
856	China Motor Bus, North Point, Hong Kong [XF98]	H44/27D	re-reg CU 8571 1982
857	China Motor Bus, North Point, Hong Kong [XF109]	H44/27D	re-reg CW 8326 1982
860	Kerrison Community Home, Thorndon	H/D	Playbus
861	London Pride Sightseeing, Rainham	O44/24D	used as a store since 1993
866	Apple Tours, New York, USA [27]	O44/26F*	re-reg BD 5303 1994 season, further re-reg BD 5301 1994
867	Apple Tours, New York, USA [8]	O44/26F*	re-reg BD 5326 1993 season, re-reg BD 5306 1994 season, further re-reg BD 5320 1994
868	London Hop-on Hop-off Service, Bermondsey	O44/24D*	
874	China Motor Bus, North Point, Hong Kong [XF94]	H44/27D	re-reg CU 7094 1982
875	China Motor Bus, North Point, Hong Kong [XF92]	H44/27D	re-reg CU 6971 1982
882	China Motor Bus, North Point, Hong Kong [XF101]	H44/27D	re-reg CV 1324 1982
883	China Motor Bus, North Point, Hong Kong [XF99]	H44/27D	re-reg CU 9676 1982
884	China Motor Bus, North Point, Hong Kong [XF105]	H44/27D	re-reg CV 6343 1982
886	London Pride Sightseeing, Rainham [306]	O45/27D	
888	China Motor Bus, North Point, Hong Kong [XF93]	H44/27D	re-reg CV 7041 1982
892	Nelson Independent Bus Services, Wickford [43]	H44/24D	
894	China Motor Bus, North Point, Hong Kong [XF118]	H44/27D	re-reg CW 648 1982
902	China Motor Bus, North Point, Hong Kong [XF141]	H44/27D	re-reg CX 3570 1982
906	China Motor Bus, North Point, Hong Kong [XF95]	H44/27D	re-reg CU 6875 1982

909	China Motor Bus, North Point, Hong Kong [XF10]	H44/27D	re-reg CW 439 1982
913	China Motor Bus, North Point, Hong Kong [XF111]	H44/27D	re-reg CM 309 1982
915	China Motor Bus, North Point, Hong Kong [XF117]	H44/27D	re-reg CW 1182 1982
919	W Jones & Son, Llanerchymedd	H44/27D	
920	London Pride Sightseeing, Rainham [220]	PO45/28D	
922	China Motor Bus, North Point, Hong Kong [XF133]	H44/27D	re-reg CW 6906 1982
924	Mike de Courcey Travel, Coventry	H44/33F	
925	London Hop-on Hop-off Service, Bermondsey	O44/31F	
926	Double Deck Coach Tours, Chicago, USA [554]	O45/28C*	re-reg 20307 H from 1992
932	China Motor Bus, North Point, Hong Kong [XF129]	H44/27D	re-reg CW 6073 1982
933	China Motor Bus, North Point, Hong Kong [XF134]	H44/27D	re-reg CW 7209 1982
934	Big Bus Company, Wimbledon	H44/27D	in store 1994
935	Apple Tours, New York, USA [7]	O45/28F*	re-reg BE 4095 1994 season
939	Double Deck Coach Tours, Chicago, USA [515]	O45/27C*	re-reg 7938 H from 1990; used for spares from 1991
941	Truronian, Truro	H44/32F	withdrawn 1994
943	China Motor Bus, North Point, Hong Kong [XF106]	H44/27D	re-reg CV 6147 1982
944	unknown owner(s), Africa	H/D	former Playbus
946	China Motor Bus, North Point, Hong Kong [XF135]	H44/27D	re-reg CW 6919 1982
948	Selkent - Plumstead [DM948]	O44/27D	
953	Apple Tours, New York, USA [3]	O45/28F*	re-reg BD 5301 1994 season, further re-reg BE 4094 1994
956	China Motor Bus, North Point, Hong Kong [XF107]	H44/27D	re-reg CV 6742 1982
962	Blue Triangle Buses, Rainham [DM962]	H44/27D	
963	London Transport Museum, Covent Garden	—	front third cut away for simulated display
968	China Motor Bus, North Point, Hong Kong [XF97]	H44/27D	re-reg CV 7978 1982
969	China Motor Bus, North Point, Hong Kong [XF120]	H44/27D	re-reg CW 4157 1982
970	Kingsley Coaches, Birtley	H45/23D	
971	China Motor Bus, North Point, Hong Kong [XF140]	H44/27D	re-reg CX 2841 1982
977	China Motor Bus, North Point, Hong Kong [XF144]	H44/27D	re-reg CY 744 1983
978	China Motor Bus, North Point, Hong Kong [XF146]	H44/27D	re-reg CY 4131 1983
979	Buffalo Travel, Flitwick [63]	H45/28D	
980	China Motor Bus, North Point, Hong Kong [XF147]	H44/27D	re-reg CY 2693 1983
983	China Motor Bus, North Point, Hong Kong [XF143]	H44/27D	re-reg CY 2240 1983
988	China Motor Bus, North Point, Hong Kong [XF149]	H44/27D	re-reg CY 3687 1983
989	China Motor Bus, North Point, Hong Kong [XF148]	H44/27D	re-reg CY 2741 1983
992	China Motor Bus, North Point, Hong Kong [XF142]	H44/27D	re-reg CY 2224 1983
995	Venture Travel, Roath	H44/27D	
998	China Motor Bus, North Point, Hong Kong [XF145]	H44/27D	re-reg CY 2009 1983
999	Shorey Travel, Maulden	H44/27D	
1002	Cherry Tree Coaches, Ruan Minor [9]	H44/24D	
1003	Brandon's of Blackmore End, near Braintree	H44/27D	
1004	Apple Tours, New York, USA [4]	O44/26F*	re-reg BD 5322 1993 season, re-reg BD 5323 1994 season, further re-reg BD 5310 1994
1007	Q-Drive Buses (London Buslines), Southall [1007]	H44/27D	
1008	Double Deck Coach Tours, Chicago, USA [551]	O45/28D	re-reg 20895 H from 1992
1013	Brandon's of Blackmore End, near Braintree	H44/27D	
1015	Apple Tours, New York, USA [18]	H45/26F*	re-reg BD 5300 1994 season, further re-reg BD 5323 1994
1020	J & J Coachlines, Herne Bay	H45/28D	
1022	Instant Muscle Ltd, Widnes	H/F	Start-up Bus for Fitness Clubs
1023	Brandon's of Blackmore End, near Braintree	H44/27D	
1029	London & Country, Reigate	H45/28D	
1031	Area Community Playbus, Downham Market	H/D	Playbus
1033	Big Bus Company, Wimbledon	O44/27D	
1037	Double Deck Coach Tours, Chicago, USA [516]	O45/25C*	re-reg 20302 H from 1992
1040	Blue Triangle Buses, Rainham [DM1040]	H44/27D	

1041	Q-Drive Buses (London Buslines), Southall [1041]	H44/27D	
1042	Geest Industries, St Lucia, Windward Islands	H44/27D	
1043	Castle Point Bus Company, Hadleigh	H45/28D	
1048	D Coaches, Morriston	H45/28D	
1050	China Motor Bus, North Point, Hong Kong [XF156]	H44/27D	re-reg CY 9201 1983
1051	Shorey Travel, Maulden	H44/32F	
1052	D Coaches, Morriston	H45/28D	
1053	China Motor Bus, North Point, Hong Kong [XF160]	H44/27D	re-reg CZ 1721 1983
1056	China Motor Bus, North Point, Hong Kong [XF159]	H44/27D	re-reg CY 8818 1983
1057	China Motor Bus, North Point, Hong Kong [XF154]	H44/27D	re-reg CY 7414 1983
1058	China Motor Bus, North Point, Hong Kong [XF152]	H44/27D	re-reg CY 6631 1983
1059	D Coaches, Morriston	H45/28D	
1063	Thurrock Swimming Club, Stanford-le-Hope	H44/27D	used for visits to other clubs
1065	China Motor Bus, North Point, Hong Kong [XF155]	H44/27D	re-reg CY 8351 1983
1066	China Motor Bus, North Point, Hong Kong [XF158]	H44/27D	re-reg CY 9924 1983
1067	Kettlewell's, Retford [8]	H45/32F	
1069	Blue Triangle Buses, Rainham	H45/28D	
1070	Bryan's of Enfield, South Mimms	H44/27D	
1071	China Motor Bus, North Point, Hong Kong [XF157]	H44/27D	re-reg CY 9643 1983
1072	Double Deck Coach Tours, Chicago, USA [526]	O45/21C*	re-reg 20305 H from 1992
1078	Big Bus Company, Wimbledon [78]	O44/27D	
1083	Blue Triangle Buses, Rainham	H44/27D	
1084	Guangzhou No 1 Bus Company, Canton, China [1375]	H45/28F*	re-reg CP 2781 1981, re-reg 01-33465 1992
1086	Bennett's Coaches, Chieveley	H44/27D	re-reg RJI 5702 1993
1087	London Borough of Richmond-upon-Thames, Twickenham [630]	H/C	Technology Unit
1090	PVS, Carlton (dealer)	O/D	for sale, former Bridge Maintenance Unit
1092	unknown owner(s), Nigeria, Africa	H/D	former Fashion Shop
1093	Apple Tours, New York, USA [12]	O44/26F*	re-reg BD 5301 1993 season, re-reg BD 5305 1994 season
1097	Brandon's of Blackmore End, near Braintree	H44/27D	
1102	Selkent - Plumstead [DM1102]	O44/27D	
1108	Isle of Wight County Council, Carisbrooke	H/D	Design & Technology Unit
1110	Blue Triangle Buses, Rainham [DM1110]	O44/27D	
1111	Blue Triangle Buses, Rainham [DM1111]	O45/27D	
1113	Double Deck Coach Tours, Chicago, USA [523]	O45/22C*	re-reg 20303 H from 1992
1114	D Coaches, Morriston	H45/28D	
1117	St Ignatius College, Enfield	H44/24D	used for excursions for pupils
1118	Apple Tours, New York, USA [20]	O45/26F*	re-reg BD 5300 1993 season, re-reg BD 5304 1994 season, further re-reg BE 4141 1994
1121	Citytours, Langridge	O45/27D	
1132	Apple Tours, New York, USA [11]	O45/26F*	re-reg BD 5323 1993 season, un-registered 1994 and used for spares
1137	Hornsby Travel Service, Ashby	H44/27D	withdrawn 1994
1141	Castle Coaches, Speke	H44/27D	
1144	D Coaches, Morriston	H45/28D	
1147	London Hop-on Hop-off Service, Bermondsey	O45/32F	
1150	London Hop-on Hop-off Service, Bermondsey	O45/32F	
1154	Castle Point Bus Company, Hadleigh	H45/28D	
1155	Home James Coach Travel, Totton	H44/27D	
1157	Double Deck Coach Tours, Chicago, USA [525]	O45/25C*	re-reg 20304 H from 1992
1159	Hoskyns Group PLC, Mayfair	H/C	Computerised Unit
1160	Dyfed Wildlife Trust, Cardigan	H/D	Marine Conservation Exhibition Unit
1175	China Motor Bus, North Point, Hong Kong [XF181]	H44/27D	re-reg DA 3973 1983
1176	Blue Triangle Buses, Rainham [DM1176]	H44/27D	
1179	Hornsby Travel Service, Ashby	H44/27D	
1180	Blue Triangle Buses, Rainham [DM1180]	H44/32F	

1181	Hornsby Travel Service, Ashby	H44/27D	
1182	China Motor Bus, North Point, Hong Kong [XF171]	H44/27D	re-reg DA 370 1983
1183	China Motor Bus, North Point, Hong Kong [XF172]	H44/27D	re-reg DA 2418 1983
1193	China Motor Bus, North Point, Hong Kong [XF173]	H44/27D	re-reg DA 1349 1983
1194	London Hop-on Hop-off Service, Bermondsey	O45/32F	
1196	China Motor Bus, North Point, Hong Kong [XF168]	H44/27D	re-reg CZ 9485 1983
1198	China Motor Bus, North Point, Hong Kong [XF169]	H44/27D	re-reg CZ 9538 1983
1203	China Motor Bus, North Point, Hong Kong [XF185]	H44/27D	re-reg DA 5811 1983
1207	China Motor Bus, North Point, Hong Kong [XF184]	H44/27D	re-reg DA 5636 1983
1209	China Motor Bus, North Point, Hong Kong [XF189]	H44/27D	re-reg DA 9108 1983
1210	China Motor Bus, North Point, Hong Kong [XF174]	H44/27D	re-reg DA 1753 1983
1211	Euroline Tours, Long Eaton	H44/28D	
1212	Post Office Corporation (London & SE Region), Kidbrooke	H/D	Exhibition Unit; withdrawn 1992 and stored
1215	China Motor Bus, North Point, Hong Kong [XF176]	H44/27D	re-reg DA 1998 1983
1216	R Bullock, Cheadle	H44/27D	
1217	Brandon's of Blackmore End, near Braintree	H44/27D	
1222	Glantawe Coaches, Pontardawe	H44/32F	
1227	Hong Kong Blood Transfusion Service, Hong Kong	H/C	Blood Collection Unit; operates on trade plates
1228	Osborne's of Tollesbury, Tollesbury [2]	H44/33F	
1234	Midland Fox, Leicester [2905]	H44/32F	
1237	D Coaches, Morriston	H44/32F	
1240	The "Collettes", Middleton	H44/OF	Lower deck used for carrying equipment
1245	Screen Facilities Ltd, Stoke Prior	H/D	Film Catering Unit
1290	Wacton Trading, Bromyard (dealer)	H/F	for sale 1994; former Playbus
1304	Guide Friday, Brighton	O44/27F	
1307	Ciba-Ceigy (UK) Ltd, Duxford	H/D	Showroom
1354	City of Birmingham Council (Social Services Department),	H/F	Playbus - named "Nellie"
1374	Film Wheels Ltd, Denham	H/F	Film Catering Unit
1414	Double Deck Coach Tours, Chicago, USA [541]	O45/27D	re-reg 20308 H from 1992
1426	Blue Triangle Buses, Rainham	H44/24D	
1441	Big Bus Company, Wimbledon	PO44/29F	
1443	Enterprise & Silver Dawn Bus Company, Waddington	H44/28D	used as a store since 1992
1447	Apple Tours, New York, USA [5]	O44/26F*	re-reg BD 5340 1993 season, re-reg BE 4128 1994 season
1449	The Harlow Majorettes, Harlow	H44/0D	Lower deck used for carrying equipment
1455	Associated Bus Ministries Trust, Surbiton [GNB1]	H/C	Promotional Unit - "The Good News Bus"
1469	Station Commercials Ltd, Brimsdown (dealer)	PO/F	for sale since 1993; former Promotional Unit
1479	Fin-Radio, Italy	H/D	Television Studio
1485	Publibus, Tallende, France	H44/24D	
1488	Big Bus Company, Wimbledon	H44/24D	
1491	Crosville Wales, Llandudno Junction [HDL921]	O44/29F	
1497	unknown owner, Tianjin, China	H45/28F*	re-reg CZ 1465 1983, re-reg 01-????? 1988
1502	unknown owner(s), Bristol	H44/29F	stored since 1990
1515	London Underground Ltd, Westminster	—	Front third of body used to form the "Supercar"
1526	Kime's Coaches, Folkingham	H44/29F	
1530	Kime's Coaches, Folkingham	H44/29F	
1532	unknown owner, Tianjin, China	H45/28F*	re-reg CN 1527 1981, re-reg 01-????? 1988
1537	Blue Triangle Buses, Rainham [DMS1537]	O44/24D	
1538	Citytours, Langridge	O44/24D	
1541	unknown owner, Tianjin, China	H45/28F*	re-reg CN 2494 1981, re-reg 01-????? 1988
1548	Big Bus Company, Wimbledon	O44/32F	
1556	unknown owner, Wuzhou, China	H45/28F*	re-reg CP 322 1981, re-reg 01-????? 1988
1562	Kowloon Motor Bus Co., Kowloon, Hong Kong [2D61]	H44/27D	re-reg CN 9710 1981; Driver Trainer since 1985
1576	Guangzhou No 1 Bus Company, Canton, China	H45/28F*	re-reg CT 7108 1982, re-reg 01-11??? 1988
1577	unknown owner, Tianjin, China	H45/28F*	re-reg CM 8371 1981, re-reg 01-????? 1988
1582	unknown owner, Wuzhou, China	H45/28F*	re-reg CN 4275 1981, re-reg 01-????? 1988

1587	unknown owner, Wuzhou, China	H45/28F*	re-reg CM 8337 1981, re-reg 01-????? 1988
1588	unknown owner, Dali, China	H45/28F*	re-reg CN 3967 1981, re-reg 01-????? 1988
1593	unknown owner, Tianjin, China	H45/28F*	re-reg CN 476 1981, re-reg 01-????? 1988
1596	Frank Ogg & Son, Aberlour	H/F	Hospitality Unit
1601	Stort Valley Coaches, Bishops Stortford	H47/32F	
1603	Mediterranea de Promociones SA, Valencia, Spain	H44/24D	Promotional & Advertisement Unit
1604	Mullany Starline, Watford	H44/24D	
1613	Magic Roundabout Company, High Wycombe	H/D	Playbus - "The Magic Bus"
1614	Eastonways, Ramsgate	H45/28D	
1616	Out House Promotions Ltd, Upper Norwood	H/D	Hospitality Unit
1619	Bennett's Coaches, Chieveley	H44/24D	re-reg RJI 5701 1993
1624	Mr Taylor, Rochford	H/D	caravan, last used in 1988
1626	London Hop-on Hop-off Service, Bermondsey	H44/23D*	
1629	Argos Bus Services, Tsing Yi, Hong Kong [5]	H59/37F	re-reg CS 2701 1981
1630	Hedingham & District, Sible Hedingham	H44/33F	
1641	Argos Bus Services, Tsing Yi, Hong Kong [8]	H59/37F	re-reg CT 4919 1982
1642	Argos Bus Services, Tsing Yi, Hong Kong [4]	H59/37F	re-reg CS 2502 1981
1644	Argos Bus Services, Tsing Yi, Hong Kong [10]	H59/37F	re-reg CT 4542 1982
1645	PC Coaches, Lincoln	H44/29F	
1647	Claireaux, Hadleigh (dealer)	H44/33F	stored since 1990
1657	Metropolitan Police Training College, Hendon	H44/32F	used for cadet training
1658	New Enterprise Coaches, Tonbridge [58]	H45/32F	
1659	PC Coaches, Lincoln	H44/29F	
1673	Radiophone Ltd, Norwich	H/D	Exhibition Unit
1678	Claireaux, Hadleigh (dealer)	H/F	used for spares since 1992; former Technology Unit
1682	Apple Tours, New York, USA [26]	H44/28F*	re-reg BD 5315 1993 season, re-reg BD 5325 1994 season, later un-registered 1994
1683	London Hop-on Hop-off Service, Bermondsey	O44/32F	
1684	Blue Triangle Buses, Rainham [D1684]	PO44/28D	
1689	Stevensons Bus Services, Spath	H/F	re-reg CBF 31Y 1983; Tree lopper
1690	Duncan's Coaches, Sawtry	H45/32F	
1691	Apple Tours, New York, USA [2]	O45/26F*	re-reg BD 5334 1993 season, re-reg BE 4140 1994 season
1692	Southern Fast Foods Ltd, Cobham	H/D	Hospitality Unit - named "Lady Louisa"
1698	Duncan's Coaches, Sawtry	H45/32F	used for spares from 1994
1701	Double Deck Coach Tours, Chicago, USA [514]	O45/24C*	re-reg 20301 H from 1992
1702	London Hop-on Hop-off Service, Bermondsey	O44/29F	
1705	Nelson Independent Bus Services, Wickford [44]	H44/27D	
1707	Brandon's of Blackmore End, near Braintree	H44/32F	
1710	Double Deck Coach Tours, Chicago, USA [528]	O45/24C*	re-reg 20306 H from 1992
1712	Normenda Coaches, Rowlands Castle	H44/27D	
1713	MDW Ltd, Paisley	H/D	Site office for building contractors
1720	Apple Tours, New York, USA [24]	O44/28F*	re-reg BD 5337 1994 season, later un-registered 1994
1721	Nelson Independent Bus Services, Wickford [35]	H45/32F	
1723	Argos Bus Services, Tsing Yi, Hong Kong [15]	H59/37F	re-reg CX 9057 1982
1726	Executive Suite Ltd, Falmouth	H/D	Hospitality Unit
1727	Argos Bus Services, Tsing Yi, Hong Kong [20]	H59/37F	re-reg CX 8509 1982
1729	Deep Purple Legionnaires, Wickford	H44/19D	Front part of lower deck used for carrying equipment
1742	Passenger Vehicle Spares, Carlton (dealer)	H/F	for sale 1994; former Film Catering Unit
1743	Argos Bus Services, Tsing Yi, Hong Kong [19]	O45/37F	re-reg CY 1311 1983
1745	Guangzhou No 1 Bus Company, Canton, China [1367]	H45/28F*	re-reg CP 1626 1981, re-reg 01-32073 1991
1746	Guangzhou No 1 Bus Company, Canton, China [1381]	H45/28F*	re-reg CX 8531 1982, re-reg 01-33459 1992
1768	Argos Bus Services, Tsing Yi, Hong Kong [18]	H59/37F	re-reg CY 316 1983
1780	Argos Bus Services, Tsing Yi, Hong Kong [14]	O59/37F	re-reg CX 7634 1982

1782	Reliance Travel, Ashton-under-Lyne	H44/32F	
1784	Argos Bus Services, Tsing Yi, Hong Kong [13]	H59/37F	re-reg CX 7602 1982
1787	Big Bus Company, Wimbledon	O44/27D	
1792	The London Bus Export Company, Chepstow (dealer)	H/D	for sale since 1993; former Library
1797	Nelson Independent Bus Services, Wickford [36]	H44/27D	
1800	Philips Consumer Electronics Ltd, Croydon	PO/F	Entertainment Centre; for sale since 1992 and stored
1802	D Coaches, Morriston	H45/28D	
1803	Nelson Independent Bus Services, Wickford [33]	H44/27D	
1810	E J Bostock & Sons, Congleton [D1]	H44/33F	
1813	London Pride Sightseeing, Rainham [303]	O45/28D	
1818	Ensign Bus Company, Rainham (dealer)	H/D	for sale 1994; former Opticians Test Centre
1819	Argos Bus Services, Tsing Yi, Hong Kong [16]	H59/37F	re-reg CY 221 1982
1825	Apple Tours, New York, USA [36]	H44/29D	un-registered 1994
1827	Crosskeys Tours, Newingreen	H45/32F	
1829	D Coaches, Morriston	H45/28D	
1830	Maybury's Coaches, Cranborne	O45/32F	used as a store since 1993
1834	Location Facilities Ltd, Feltham	H/D	Film Catering Unit
1836	Apple Tours, New York, USA [29]	O45/28F*	re-reg BD 5341 1994 season
1837	Bodegas Los Oteros, Spain	H44/24D	
1838	Gray Line Tours, Maynooth, Eire	H44/27D	re-reg 7997 ZW 1986
1839	Apple Tours, New York, USA [10]	O44/26F*	re-reg BD 5341 1993 season, re-reg BD 5326 1994 season
1840	Salford Community Transport, Salford	H/D	Playbus
1842	Surrey University, Guildford	H/D	Technology Unit
1845	Mr R Wright, Rainham (dealer)	H44/24D	for sale since 1993
1850	Surrey Health Leisure Services, Camberley	H/D	Playbus
1854	Westring's Coaches, West Wittering	H44/24D	
1855	Truronian, Truro	H44/24D	
1867	Blue Triangle Buses, Rainham [DMS1867]	H44/24D	
1868	Leaside Buses - Stamford Hill [DMS1868]	H44/24D	
1871	Liverpool Community Transport, Liverpool	H/D	Technology Teaching Unit; stored since 1990
1873	Apple Tours, New York, USA [15]	O44/26F*	re-reg BD 5306 1993 season, re-reg BD 5325 1994 season
1874	Castle Coaches, Speke	H44/24D	
1877	London Borough of Tower Hamlets, Shadwell	H/D	Playbus
1878	Argos Bus Services, Tsing Yi, Hong Kong [17]	H59/37F	re-reg CX 8806 1982
1880	D Coaches, Morriston	H45/28D	
1882	London & Country, Reigate	H44/24D	
1887	unknown owner, Eton Wick	H44/24D	unused since 1987; for sale 1994
1890	Bryan's of Enfield, South Mimms	H44/24D	
1892	Apple Tours, New York, USA [31]	H45/28F*	re-reg BD 5322 1994 season
1893	Shorey Travel, Maulden	H45/32F	re-reg DDA 66 1984
1896	Smith's (Your Bus), Alcester [45]	H44/24D	
1898	Glenvic of Bristol, Bishopsworth	H45/25D	
1907	Community Links, London E6	H/D	Advice Centre; stored since 1990
1908	Midland Fox, Leicester [2892]	H44/32F	
1911	Omegaland Racing, Weston-Super-Mare	H/D	Hospitality Unit
1915	East Yorkshire Motor Services, Kingston-upon-Hull [895]	H44/29F	
1923	Buzz Discotheque, Southend-on-Sea	PO/D	Promotional Unit; stored since 1993
1927	Midland Fox, Leicester [2897]	H44/32F	used for spares since 1993
1929	Apple Tours, New York, USA [9]	O44/26F*	used for spares since 1993
1935	London Hop-on Hop-off Service, Bermondsey	O44/28F*	fitted with blue canvas roof
1941	Castle Point Bus Company, Hadleigh	H45/32F	
1942	Mr D Chaffe, Edingworth	H/D	Classroom for "Project Otter"; for sale 1994
1943	Philips Consumer Electronics Ltd, Croydon	PO/F	Entertainment Centre; for sale since 1992 and stored

1944	London Hop-on Hop-off Service, Bermondsey	O44/33F	
1948	Dewsway, Somersham	H44/24D	
1949	Double Deck Coach Tours, Chicago, USA [553]	H45/28D	Used for spares since 1991
1952	PVS, Carlton (dealer)	PO/D	for sale 1994; former Overhead Maintenance & Towing Vehicle
1955	Kent County Constabulary, Maidstone	H/F	Exhibition Unit
1958	Big Bus Company, Wimbledon	O45/32F	
1962	London Hop-on Hop-off Service, Bermondsey	O44/32F	
1967	Hutchison Telecommunications Ltd, Hertford	H/D	Promotional Unit; re-reg HTL 446 1992
1968	D R Grasby, Oxhill	H44/29F	Rolls Royce engine fitted 1976, Gardner engine fitted 1993
1969	Mayne's of Manchester, Clayton [10]	H45/32F	
1971	London Hop-on Hop-off Service, Bermondsey	O45/32F	
1972	Hornsby Travel Service, Ashby	H44/27D	used as a store since 1990
1977	Apple Tours, New York, USA [16]	O45/26F*	re-reg BD 5304 1993 season, re-reg BE 4135 1994 season
1979	Big Bus Company, Wimbledon [979]	PO44/24D	
1981	UK Gas Appliance Advisory Service, Turkey	H/D	Promotional Unit; re-reg 1 NTG 1985, re-reg MMK 668P 1990
1982	Apple Tours, New York, USA [30]	O45/28F*	re-reg BD 5341 1994 season, further re-reg BD 5304 1994
1983	Higgs & Hill PLC, New Malden	H/F	Construction Regulations Training Bus
1984	Apple Tours, New York, USA [19]	H45/26F*	un-registered 1994
1988	Post Office Corporation (London & SE Region), Kidbrooke	H/F	Exhibition Unit; withdrawn 1992 and stored
1989	Red & Green Coaches, Dartford Heath	H45/32F	
1991	Kingsley Coaches, Birtley	H44/32F	
1997	Acton Coaches, Wrexham	H44/29F	
2001	Regency Tours, Bath	O44/24D	
2002	H A Scutt, Owston Ferry	H44/29F	
2005	Post Office Corporation (London & SE Region), Kidbrooke	H/F	Exhibition & Sales Unit; withdrawn 1992 and stored
2009	Midland Fox, Leicester [2914]	H44/32F	
2011	D Coaches, Morriston	H44/32F	
2012	Cook's Travel, Biggleswade	H44/29F	
2019	Kingsley Coaches, Birtley	H44/32F	
2021	London Hop-on Hop-off Service, Bermondsey	O44/29F	
2023	Mr R Wright, Rainham (dealer)	PO/D	stored since 1993; former Hospitality Unit
2024	Regis Coaches, Challow	H45/32F	
2029	London Pride Sightseeing, Rainham [229]	PO45/31F	
2030	Filer's Travel, Ilfracombe	H44/24D	
2033	Big Bus Company, Wimbledon	O44/35F	
2034	Midland Fox, Leicester [2934]	H44/29F	
2035	Mayne's of Manchester, Clayton [5]	H45/32F	
2036	London Pride Sightseeing, Rainham [236]	PO45/31F	
2037	West Midlands Travel, Birmingham [2037]	H45/32F	stored since 1992
2038	Fourways Coaches, Chelmsford	H45/32F	
2039	Fareway Passenger Services, Kirkby [154]	H44/32F	
2042	Midland Red (South), Rugby [954]	H44/29F	
2044	Midland Red (South), Rugby [952]	H44/29F	
2045	Yellow Buses, Bournemouth [530]	H44/32F	
2046	D S Kerr, Galston	H45/29F	
2047	Midland Fox, Leicester [2947]	H44/29F	
2048	D S Kerr, Galston	H44/32F	
2049	Buffalo Travel, Flitwick [72]	H44/32F	
2052	unknown owner(s), Avon	H/D	Staff bus for construction workers
2054	S J Research Ltd, Cambridge	H/D	Exhibition Unit
2056	Mr T Wigley, Carlton (dealer)	H45/25D	for sale 1994

2057	Marbill Coach Services, Beith	H44/32F	
2058	Regis Coaches, Challow	H45/32F	
2060	China Motor Bus, North Point, Hong Kong [XF197]	H44/27D	re-reg DD 5326 1984
2061	London Pride Sightseeing, Rainham [361]	O45/29F	
2066	London Hop-on Hop-off Service, Bermondsey	H44/32F	
2069	Green Lane Travel, Brent	H45/32F	
2076	China Motor Bus, North Point, Hong Kong [XF195]	H44/27D	re-reg DD 4682 1984
2077	Green Lane Travel, Brent	H44/24D	
2080	Village Group, Garston [V18]	H44/24D	
2082	London Hop-on Hop-off Service, Bermondsey	O44/26F*	
2083	China Motor Bus, North Point, Hong Kong [XF193]	H44/27D	re-reg DD 1296 1984
2086	China Motor Bus, North Point, Hong Kong [XF192]	H44/27D	re-reg DD 1471 1984
2088	Kent County Constabulary, Maidstone	H/F	Exhibition Unit
2089	Ripley, Carlton (dealer)	H44/24D	for sale 1994
2091	London Pride Sightseeing, Rainham [291]	PO45/29F	
2093	China Motor Bus, North Point, Hong Kong [XF194]	H44/27D	re-reg DD 4638 1984
2094	Dewsway, Somersham	H44/33F	
2096	China Motor Bus, North Point, Hong Kong [FC1]	DP44/27D	re-reg DD 7785 1984
2097	China Motor Bus, North Point, Hong Kong [XF198]	H44/27D	re-reg DD 5682 1984
2101	Apple Tours, New York [38]	O45/29F	un-registered 1994
2104	London Pride Sightseeing, Rainham [204]	PO45/29F	
2105	China Motor Bus, North Point, Hong Kong [XF196]	H44/27D	re-reg DD 5273 1984
2109	Big Bus Company, Wimbledon	O45/28D	
2114	China Motor Bus, North Point, Hong Kong [XF204]	H44/27D	re-reg DD 5513 1984
2119	Apple Tours, New York, USA [21]	H44/28F*	re-reg BD 5315 1994 season
2123	Argos Bus Services, Tsing Yi, Hong Kong [30]	H59/36F	re-reg DD 2113 1984
2124	Argos Bus Services, Tsing Yi, Hong Kong [31]	H59/36F	re-reg DD 2972 1984
2126	Hedingham & District, Sible Hedingham	H45/34F	
2127	London Pride Sightseeing, Rainham [327]	O45/29F	
2128	Jolly Roger, Towthorpe	H45/32F	named "Captain Hook"
2129	Mike de Courcey Travel, Coventry	H44/32F	
2130	Guangzhou No 1 Bus Company, Canton, China [1358]	H45/28F*	re-reg DB 7404 1984, re-reg 01-32068 1991
2131	Mayne's of Manchester, Clayton [1]	H44/29F	
2133	Midland Fox, Leicester [2933]	H44/29F	
2134	Guangzhou No 1 Bus Company, Canton, China [1368]	H45/28F*	re-reg DB 6725 1984, re-reg 01-32075 1991
2136	Midland Red (South), Rugby [955]	H44/29F	
2137	West Midlands Travel, Birmingham [2137]	H44/33F	stored since 1992
2138	Selwyn Motors, Belton	H45/32F	
2140	Argos Bus Services, Tsing Yi, Hong Kong [72]	H59/36F	re-reg DM 3554 1986, re-reg EM 3585 1990; used as a rest room since 1992
2141	Buffalo Travel, Flitwick [71]	H44/32F	
2142	Guangzhou No 1 Bus Company, Canton, China [1366]	H45/28F*	re-reg CZ 8823 1983, re-reg 01-32071 1991
2143	Mullany Starline, Watford	H45/28D	
2145	Argos Bus Services, Tsing Yi, Hong Kong [73]	H45/28D	re-reg CZ 5855 1983
2146	Guangzhou No 1 Bus Company, Canton, China [1387]	H45/28F*	re-reg CZ 8526 1983, re-reg 01-33??? 1992
2147	Argos Bus Services, Tsing Yi, Hong Kong [68]	H45/28D	re-reg DA 1262 1983
2149	Guangzhou No 1 Bus Company, Canton, China [1364]	H45/28F*	re-reg DB 2378 1984, re-reg 01-32072 1991
2150	Guangzhou No 1 Bus Company, Canton, China [1374]	H45/28F*	re-reg CZ 4529 1983, re-reg 01-33466 1992
2151	Swanbrook Transport, Cheltenham	H44/29F	
2152	Dewsway, Somersham	H45/32F	
2153	Argos Bus Services, Tsing Yi, Hong Kong [74]	H45/28D	re-reg DA 8570 1984
2155	Guangzhou No 1 Bus Company, Canton, China [1376]	H45/28F*	re-reg CZ 8621 1983, re-reg 01-33464 1992
2157	Argos Bus Services, Tsing Yi, Hong Kong [70]	H45/28D	re-reg DA 1980 1983
2161	James Brown & Son (A1 Service), Dreghorn	H45/32F	
2162	James Brown & Son (A1 Service), Dreghorn	H45/32F	
2163	Mayne's of Manchester, Clayton [3]	H44/29F	
2165	Guangzhou No 1 Bus Company, Canton, China [1359]	H45/28F*	re-reg DA 7341 1984, re-reg 01-32067 1991

2167	Castle Point Bus Company, Hadleigh	H45/25D	used for spares since 1993
2168	London Northern - Holloway [DMS2168]	H44/24D	
2171	Guangzhou No 1 Bus Company, Canton, China [1363]	H45/28F*	re-reg CZ 9141 1983, re-reg 01-32076 1991
2173	Apple Tours, New York, USA [34]	H45/25D	un-registered 1994
2174	Glyndwr Soaring Club, Denbeigh	H45/32F	Observation and Control Tower
2175	Jolly Roger, Towthorpe	H45/32F	named "Captain Billy Bones"
2177	London Borough of Haringey, London N17 [9191]	H/DL	Exhibition Unit; stored since 1993
2178	Guangzhou No 1 Bus Company, Canton, China [1360]	H45/28F*	re-reg DB 7078 1984, re-reg 01-32066 1991
2182	Apple Tours, New York, USA [22]	H44/28F*	re-reg BD 5310 1993 season, re-reg BD 5322 1994 season, further re-reg BD 5324 1994
2185	Pride of the Clyde Coaches, Port Glasgow	H44/32F	
2186	Clynnog & Trefor Motor Company, Trefor	H45/32F	
2187	Circle Line Coach & Omnibus Company, Gloucester	H44/24D	
2188	Apple Tours, New York, USA [25]	H44/28F*	re-reg BD 5326 1994 season later un-registered 1994
2190	Yellow Buses, Bournemouth [531]	H44/32F	
2191	Yellow Buses, Bournemouth [532]	H44/32F	
2192	Morley's of Whittlesey, Whittlesey	H45/32F	
2193	Maybury's Coaches, Cranborne	O44/32F	used as a store since 1993
2194	Fareway Passenger Services, Kirkby [149]	H44/32F	
2195	Eastern Counties, Norwich [D505]	H45/32F	
2196	Howell's of Bargoed, Deri	H45/32F	
2198	Metrobus, Orpington	H45/25D	
2199	Circle Line Coach & Omnibus Company, Gloucester	H43/33F	
2200	Mikro Coaches of Crewe, Shavington	H45/25D	
2202	Wealden PSV Sales, Five Oak Green (dealer)	H45/32F	for sale 1994
2203	Fareway Passenger Services, Kirkby [150]	H44/32F	
2205	Big Bus Company, Wimbledon	O44/24D	Leyland engine fitted 1990
2206	The London Bus Export Company, Chepstow (dealer)	H/F	for sale and stored since 1993; former Exhibition Unit
2207	Guangzhou No 1 Bus Company, Canton, China [1382]	H45/28F*	re-reg DK 5210 1986, re-reg 01-33458 1992
2208	Circle Line Coach & Omnibus Company, Gloucester	H44/24D	
2210	Wealden PSV Sales, Five Oak Green (dealer)	H45/32F	for sale 1994
2211	Eastonways, Ramsgate	H45/25D	
2212	Beeston's, Hadleigh	H44/28D	
2213	Wealden PSV Sales, Five Oak Green (dealer)	H45/32F	for sale 1994
2215	Wealden PSV Sales, Five Oak Green (dealer)	H45/32F	for sale 1994
2216	Keystone Coaches, Thrapston	H44/28D	
2218	Argos Bus Services, Tsing Yi, Hong Kong [71]	H45/28D	re-reg DH 1349 1985, re-reg EM 3872 1990
2219	Highland Scottish Omnibuses, Inverness [D219]	H45/29F	
2220	Wealden PSV Sales, Five Oak Green (dealer)	H45/32F	for sale 1994
2221	Ron's Coaches, Ashington	H44/28D	
2223	Farleigh Coaches, Wouldham	H44/24D	withdrawn 1994
2224	Fareway Passenger Services, Kirkby [157]	H44/32F	
2225	Yellow Buses, Bournemouth [533]	H44/32F	
2231	Yellow Buses, Bournemouth [534]	H44/32F	
2232	Morley's of Whittlesey, Whittlesey	H45/32F	
2234	Howell's of Bargoed, Deri	H45/32F	
2235	Eastonways, Ramsgate	H44/28D	
2236	Fuggles of Benenden, Benenden	H45/32F	
2238	University of the South Bank, London SE1	H/C	Information Technology Unit
2239	Howell's of Bargoed, Deri	H45/32F	
2241	Midland Red (South), Rugby [953]	H44/29F	
2242	Verwood & District Coaches, Verwood	H44/32F	
2243	Metrobus, Orpington	H45/25D	
2245	Fareway Passenger Services, Kirkby [152]	H44/32F	
2246	unknown museum, near Bordeaux, France	H44/24D	static exhibit

2247	Big Bus Company, Wimbledon [247]	O44/24D	
2249	R Bullock, Cheadle	H44/24D	Iveco engine fitted 1989
2253	Victory Tours, Sixpenny Handley	H44/24D	
2254	Blue Triangle Buses, Rainham	H44/24D	Iveco engine fitted 1988; withdrawn 1994
2255	Flittner & Marx, Grosswaldstudt, Germany	H44/24D	Iveco engine fitted 1989
2256	McColl's Coaches, Balloch	H44/24D	Iveco engine fitted 1989
2257	London General - Putney [DMT2257]	H/D	Iveco engine fitted 1989; Driver Trainer from 1992
2260	R Bullock, Cheadle	H44/24D	Iveco engine fitted 1988; used for spares since 1994
2261	Stuart Palmer Travel, Dunstable	H44/24D	Iveco engine fitted 1989
2264	Blue Triangle Buses, Rainham	H44/24D	Iveco engine fitted 1989; withdrawn 1994
2266	Len Hopkins Coaches, Ogmore Vale	H44/24D	
2267	Kinchbus, Barrow-upon-Soar	H44/24D	Iveco engine fitted 1989
2271	Blue Triangle Buses, Rainham [DMS2271]	O44/24D	Iveco engine fitted 1988
2272	R Bullock, Cheadle	H44/24D	Gardner engine fitted 1993
2273	Venture Travel, Roath	H44/24D	Iveco engine fitted 1989
2275	Glaxo Group Research, Stevenage	H44/24D	Iveco engine fitted 1989; Internal staff transport
2276	Fareway Passenger Services, Kirkby	H44/24D	used for spares since 1993
2280	unknown owner, China	H44/24D	Iveco engine fitted 1989; re-reg 01-????? 1994
2281	London General - Putney [DMS2281]	H44/24D	Iveco engine fitted 1987; Driver Trainer from 1992
2282	The Gedney Partnership, Southfleet	H44/24D	Iveco engine fitted 1989; Staff transport for farm workers
2283	London General - Merton [DMT2283]	H/D	Iveco engine fitted 1988; Driver Trainer from 1992
2285	Stort Valley Coaches, Bishops Stortford	H44/24D	Iveco engine fitted 1989
2286	Midland Fox, Leicester [2986]	H44/24D	Iveco engine fitted 1989
2289	Bryan Garratt Coach Travel, Glenfield	H44/24D	Iveco engine fitted 1989
2290	London General - Merton [DMT2290]	H/D	Iveco engine fitted 1988; Driver Trainer from 1992
2291	Leaside Buses - Stamford Hill [DMS2291]	O44/28D	
2292	Arkleston Coaches, Renfrew	H44/24D	
2299	Enterprise Safety Coaches, Chatteris	H44/24D	used for spares since 1992
2303	Mayne's of Manchester, Clayton [33]	H44/31F	
2304	London General - Putney [DMT2304]	H/D	Iveco engine fitted 1988; Driver Trainer from 1992
2305	Tellings-Golden Miller, Grangetown [60]	H44/24D	
2308	Flittner & Marx, Grosswaldstudt, Germany	H44/24D	Iveco engine fitted 1989
2311	Midland Fox, Leicester [2971]	H44/24D	Iveco engine fitted 1988
2312	Stuart Palmer Travel, Dunstable	H44/24D	Iveco engine fitted 1989
2314	Blue Triangle Buses, Rainham	H44/24D	Iveco engine fitted 1989
2315	Victory Tours, Sixpenny Handley	H44/24D	
2321	Busybus, Hemel Hempstead	H44/24D	
2322	Mayne's of Manchester, Clayton [7]	H44/31F	
2324	Hedingham & District, Sible Hedingham	H44/24D	
2326	Big Bus Company, Wimbledon [326]	O44/24D	
2332	Stuart Palmer Travel, Dunstable	H44/24D	Iveco engine fitted 1988
2333	Fleetline Buses, South Mimms	H44/24D	Iveco engine fitted 1989
2336	Stuart Palmer Travel, Dunstable	H44/24D	Iveco engine fitted 1989
2337	Blue Triangle Buses, Rainham	H44/24D	Iveco engine fitted 1989
2340	Kinchbus, Barrow-upon-Soar	H44/24D	Iveco engine fitted 1989
2342	unknown owner, China	H44/24D	Iveco engine fitted 1989; re-reg 01-????? 1994
2345	Stuart Palmer Travel, Dunstable	H44/24D	Iveco engine fitted 1988
2347	London General - Merton [DMT2347]	H/D	Iveco engine fitted 1989; Driver Trainer from 1992
2351	London General - Putney [DMT2351]	H/D	Iveco engine fitted 1988; Driver Trainer from 1992

2354	Venture Travel, Roath	H44/24D	Iveco engine fitted 1987
2357	Shorey Travel, Maulden	H44/27D	
2361	Big Bus Company, Wimbledon	PO44/24D	
2363	Stuart Palmer Travel, Dunstable	H44/24D	Iveco engine fitted 1989
2365	Big Bus Company, Wimbledon	O44/24D	
2366	Midland Fox, Leicester [2955]	H44/24D	Iveco engine fitted 1989
2367	London General - Putney [DMT2367]	H/D	Iveco engine fitted 1988; Driver Trainer from 1992
2368	Stuart Palmer Travel, Dunstable	H44/24D	Iveco engine fitted 1989
2374	Speedybus Services, Kowloon, Hong Kong (dealer)	H44/24D	Iveco engine fitted 1987; storeroom since 1993
2375	Venture Travel, Roath	H44/24D	Iveco engine fitted 1989
2376	Bryan Garratt Coach Travel, Glenfield	H44/29D	Iveco engine fitted 1987
2379	Midland Fox, Leicester [2979]	H44/24D	Iveco engine fitted 1989
2383	Castle Point Bus Company, Hadleigh	H44/27D	Iveco engine fitted 1989
2384	London General - Merton [DMT2384]	H/D	Iveco engine fitted 1988; Driver Trainer from 1992
2386	Blue Triangle Buses, Rainham	H44/24D	Iveco engine fitted 1989; withdrawn 1994
2389	Eastonways, Ramsgate	H44/24D	
2390	Eastonways, Ramsgate	H44/30F	
2391	Blue Triangle Buses, Rainham [DM2391]	O44/24D	Iveco engine fitted 1989, Gardner engine fitted 1992
2394	Midland Fox, Leicester [2994]	H44/24D	Iveco engine fitted 1988
2395	Crown Line Coaches, Ware	H44/24D	
2396	Eastonways, Ramsgate	H44/24D	
2397	London General - Merton [DMT2397]	H/D	Iveco engine fitted 1988; Driver Trainer from 1992
2401	Worth's Coaches, Enstone	H44/24D	
2402	unknown owner(s), Lyon, France	H44/24D	Iveco engine fitted 1989
2405	Kinchbus, Barrow-upon-Soar	H44/24D	Iveco engine fitted 1989; withdrawn 1994
2407	Apple Tours, New York, USA [23]	H44/28F*	Gardner engine fitted 1984; re-reg BD 5303 1993 season, re-reg BD 5310 1994 season, further re-reg BD 5334 1994
2411	Fleetline Buses, South Mimms	H44/24D	Iveco engine fitted 1989
2412	Big Bus Company, Wimbledon [412]	O44/24D	
2413	London General - Merton [DMT2413]	H/D	Iveco engine fitted 1989; Driver Trainer from 1992
2414	Midland Fox, Leicester [2964]	H44/24D	Iveco engine fitted 1989
2417	Kinchbus, Barrow-upon-Soar	H44/24D	Iveco engine fitted 1989; used for spares from 1994
2419	Len Hopkins Coaches, Ogmore Vale	H44/24D	
2422	Victory Tours, Sixpenny Handley	H44/24D	
2423	Stuart Palmer Travel, Dunstable	H44/24D	Iveco engine fitted 1989; used for spares from 1993
2425	Stuart Palmer Travel, Dunstable	H44/24D	Iveco engine fitted 1989
2426	Speedybus Services, Kowloon, Hong Kong (dealer)	H44/24D	Iveco engine fitted 1989; for sale since 1993
2428	St Vincents Primary School, Dagenham	H/D	Iveco engine fitted 1988, engine removed 1993; static playbus
2432	Marine Land Theme Park, Barcelona, Spain	H44/24D	Iveco engine fitted 1988; Courtesy Bus
2434	Kinchbus, Barrow-upon-Soar	H44/24D	Iveco engine fitted 1989
2435	Marine Land Theme Park, Barcelona, Spain	H44/24D	Iveco engine fitted 1988; Courtesy Bus
2438	Blue Triangle Buses, Rainham	H44/24D	Iveco engine fitted 1989
2441	Marine Land Theme Park, Barcelona, Spain	H44/24D	Iveco engine fitted 1989; Courtesy Bus
2444	Kinchbus, Barrow-upon-Soar	H44/24D	Iveco engine fitted 1989; withdrawn 1994
2445	London General - Putney [DMS2445]	H44/24D	Iveco engine fitted 1989; Driver Trainer from 1992
2446	Aylesbury Vale Youth for Christ, Stoke Mandeville	H44/24D	Publicity & Touring Bus
2447	Big Bus Company, Wimbledon	O44/25D	

2448	Bordabus, Woodford	H44/24D	Iveco engine fitted 1988
2450	Kinchbus, Barrow-upon-Soar	H44/24D	Iveco engine fitted 1988, withdrawn 1994
2453	Cheerroute Ltd, Rainham (dealer)	H44/24D	used for spares since 1993
2454	London Bus Sales Ltd, Fulwell (dealer)	H44/24D	for sale since 1993
2455	Kinchbus, Barrow-upon-Soar	H44/24D	Iveco engine fitted 1988
2456	Mr G Laming, Coulsdon	H41/23D	Iveco engine fitted 1989; Preserved
2457	R Bullock, Cheadle	H44/24D	used for spares since 1992
2462	Venture Travel, Roath	H44/24D	Iveco engine fitted 1988
2463	Motts Coaches (Yellow Bus), Stoke Mandeville [463]	H44/24D	
2466	unknown owner, China	H44/24D	Iveco engine fitted 1989; re-reg 01-????? 1994
2468	Buffalo Travel, Flitwick [68]	H44/24D	
2469	Regency Tours, Bath	H44/24D	Iveco engine fitted 1989
2472	Mary How Trust for Cancer Prevention, Pulborough	H/Ft	Health Clinic
2473	Midland Fox, Leicester [2973]	H44/24D	Iveco engine fitted 1987
2474	Len Hopkins Coaches, Ogmore Vale	H44/24D	
2476	London General - Merton [DMT2476]	H/D	Iveco engine fitted 1988; Driver Trainer from 1992
2477	Midland Fox, Leicester [2977]	H44/24D	Iveco engine fitted 1989
2478	P & R Coaches, Penwortham	H44/24D	
2480	Stuart Palmer Travel, Dunstable	H44/24D	Iveco engine fitted 1987
2481	Stuart Palmer Travel, Dunstable	H44/24D	Iveco engine fitted 1988
2484	Bryan Garratt Coach Travel, Glenfield	H44/24D	Iveco engine fitted 1989
2488	Decker Autosales, Treforest	H/C	Static site office
2489	London General - Merton [DMT2489]	H/D	Iveco engine fitted 1988; Driver Trainer from 1992
2492	Glaxo Group Research, Stevenage	H44/24D	Iveco engine fitted 1989; Internal staff transport
2493	Buffalo Travel, Flitwick [64]	H44/24D	Iveco engine fitted 1989
2494	unknown owner, China	H44/24D	Iveco engine fitted 1989; re-reg 01-????? 1994
2495	Midland Fox, Leicester [2995]	H44/24D	Iveco engine fitted 1989
2497	unknown owner, China	H44/24D	Iveco engine fitted 1989; re-reg 01-????? 1994
2498	Big Bus Company, Wimbledon	H44/24D	in store 1994
2499	Castle Point Bus Company, Hadleigh	H44/27D	stored since 1993
2500	Kinchbus, Barrow-upon-Soar	H44/24D	Iveco engine fitted 1989
2501	Midland Fox, Leicester [2991]	H44/24D	Iveco engine fitted 1987
2502	unknown owner, China	H44/24D	Iveco engine fitted 1989; re-reg 01-????? 1994
2503	Mr R Wright, Rainham (dealer)	H44/24D	for sale since 1992
2505	J D Transport Ltd, Heathrow	H/D	Film Catering Unit
2506	Verwood & District Coaches, Verwood	H44/24D	withdrawn 1994
2509	Bryan's of Enfield, South Mimms	H44/32F	Iveco engine fitted 1989; withdrawn 1994
2512	Geoff Ripley, Carlton (dealer)	H44/24D	Iveco engine fitted 1989; held for re-sale to Hong Kong 1994
2513	Enterprise Safety Coaches, Chatteris	H44/24D	Iveco engine fitted 1989
2514	unknown owner, China	H44/24D	Iveco engine fitted 1989; re-reg 01-????? 1994
2515	Mayne's of Manchester, Clayton [2]	H44/31F	
2523	Stuart Palmer Travel, Dunstable	H44/25D	Iveco engine fitted 1989
2524	Kime's Coaches, Folkingham	H44/24D	Iveco engine fitted 1988 , Gardner engine fitted 1992
2525	Stuart Palmer Travel, Dunstable	H44/24D	Iveco engine fitted 1987
2526	Midland Fox, Leicester [2956]	H44/24D	Iveco engine fitted 1988
2531	Eastern Counties, Norwich [DD504]	H44/27D	
2533	Buffalo Travel, Flitwick [65]	H44/27D	Iveco engine fitted 1989
2534	Tigerways, Harlow	H44/27D	
2538	John Boyce, Milton of Campsie	H44/27D	Iveco engine fitted 1988
2539	R Bullock, Cheadle	H44/27D	Gardner engine fitted 1993
2541	Midland Fox, Leicester [2941]	H44/27D	Iveco engine fitted 1989
2542	Hornsby Travel Service, Ashby	H44/27D	
2545	Big Bus Company, Wimbledon	PO44/27D	

2548	Midland Fox, Leicester [2984]	H44/27D	Iveco engine fitted 1989
2553	Midland Fox, Leicester [2953]	H44/27D	Iveco engine fitted 1989
2554	Midland Fox, Leicester [2954]	H44/27D	Iveco engine fitted 1989
2555	Mayne's of Manchester, Clayton [35]	H44/31F	
2556	London Northern - Holloway [D2556]	O44/27D	
2559	Vodac Vodaphones Ltd, Newbury	H/D	Exhibition Unit
2560	Stuart Palmer Travel, Dunstable	H44/27D	Iveco engine fitted 1988
2563	R Bullock, Cheadle	H44/27D	Gardner engine fitted 1993
2566	Midland Fox, Leicester [2966]	H44/27D	Iveco engine fitted 1989
2569	Midland Fox, Leicester [2969]	H44/27D	Iveco engine fitted 1988
2573	Eastern Counties, Norwich [DD506]	H44/27D	
2576	Tigerways, Harlow	H44/27D	
2579	Mayne's of Manchester, Clayton [9]	H44/27F	
2580	Shorey Travel, Maulden	H44/27D	
2582	Midland Fox, Leicester [2982]	H44/27D	Iveco engine fitted 1989
2583	Arkleston Coaches, Renfrew	H44/27D	
2588	Midland Fox, Leicester [2988]	H44/27D	Iveco engine fitted 1989
2590	Blue Triangle Buses, Rainham [DMS2590]	H44/27D	
2592	On Set Location Services, Norwich	H/D	Film Catering Unit
2593	Arkleston Coaches, Renfrew	H44/27D	
2594	Mayne's of Manchester, Clayton [34]	H44/31F	
2595	Big Bus Company, Wimbledon [595]	O44/27D	
2600	John Penfold School, Harefield	H44/27D	School Transport
2601	Mayne's of Manchester, Clayton [31]	H44/31F	
2605	Midland Fox, Leicester [2965]	H44/27D	Iveco engine fitted 1989
2609	unknown owner, China	H44/27D	Iveco engine fitted 1989; re-reg 01-????? 1994
2610	Midland Fox, Leicester [2960]	H44/27D	Iveco engine fitted 1988
2612	Midland Fox, Leicester [2962]	H44/27D	Iveco engine fitted 1988
2618	Merseyside Transport, Liverpool	H44/27D	stored, not used since 1992
2619	Mayne's of Manchester, Clayton [19]	H44/31F	
2625	Enterprise Safety Coaches, Chatteris	H44/27D	Iveco engine fitted 1989
2629	Arsenal F.C. Stadium Museum, Highbury (body only)	—	Iveco engine fitted 1987, and removed 1993; Static display
2633	See More Travel, London N17	H44/27D	Iveco engine fitted 1988; re-reg WLT 916 1992; re-reg DGJ 415S 1993
2634	Filer's Travel, Ilfracombe	H44/27D	Iveco engine fitted 1989
2636	Midland Fox, Leicester [2976]	H44/27D	Iveco engine fitted 1988
2639	Blue Triangle Buses, Rainham	H44/27D	Iveco engine fitted 1988; withdrawn 1994
2641	East Sussex Fire Brigade Training Centre, Maresfield	H44/27D	Iveco engine fitted 1988; used for training and recovery exercises since 1993
2642	Midland Fox, Leicester [2942]	H44/27D	Iveco engine fitted 1989
2643	Kinchbus, Barrow-upon-Soar	H44/27D	Iveco engine fitted 1989; withdrawn 1994
2646	Arrow Travel, Pulborough	H44/27D	Iveco engine fitted 1988

* Fitted with offside doors.

APPENDIX TWO Summary of the D/DM/DMS Family as Built

Fleet Numbers:	Registrations:	Delivered:	Body:	Engine:
DMS 1-131	EGP1-131J	10/70-6/71	PRV	Gardner
DMS 132	EGP132J	7/71	PRV	Leyland
DMS 133-136	EGP133-136J	6/71-7/71	PRV	Gardner
DMS 137-414	JGF137-414K	7/71-6/72	PRV	Gardner
DMS 415-494	MLK415-494L	6/72-11/72	PRV	Gardner
DMS 495-607	MLK495-607L	10/72-3/73	PRV	Leyland
DMS 608-611	MLK608-611L	3/73-4/73	PRV	Gardner
DMS 612-616	MLK612-616L	4/73	PRV	Leyland
DMS 617-619	MLK617-619L	4/73	PRV	Gardner
DMS 620-636	MLK620-636L	4/73-5/73	PRV	Leyland
DMS 637-639	MLK637-639L	5/73	PRV	Gardner
DMS 640-654	MLK640-654L	5/73	PRV	Leyland
DMS 655	MLK655L	7/73	PRV	Gardner
DMS 656-658	MLK656-658L	5/73	PRV	Leyland
DMS 659-660	MLK659-660L	7/73	PRV	Gardner
DMS 661-695	MLK661-695L	6/73-7/73	PRV	Leyland
DMS 696-853	TGX696-853L	7/73-4/74	PRV	Leyland
DMS 854	TGX854M	4/74	PRV	Leyland (B20)
DMS 855-863	TGX855-863M	4/74-5/74	PRV	Leyland
DMS 864	TGX864M	5/74	PRV	Rolls-Royce
DMS 865-900	TGX865-900M	5/74-7/74	PRV	Leyland
DMS 901-917	SMU901-917N	7/74-8/74	PRV	Leyland
DM 918-947	SMU918-947N	8/74-9/74	PRV	Leyland
DM 948-999	GHV948-999N	9/74-12/74	PRV	Leyland
DM 1000	GHV500N	12/74	PRV	Leyland
DM 1001-1124	GHV1-124N	11/74-7/75	PRV	Leyland
DM 1125-1198	KUC125-198P	7/75-1/76	PRV	Leyland
DM 1199	KUC199P	11/75	PRV	Rolls-Royce
DM 1200-1217	KUC200-217P	11/75-3/76	PRV	Leyland
DM 1218-1247	KUC218-247P	1/76-4/76	MCW	Leyland
DMS 1248-1297	JGU248-297K	3/72-7/72	MCW	Gardner
DMS 1298-1371	MLH298-371L	7/72-12/72	MCW	Gardner
DMS 1372-1451	MLH372-451L	11/72-5/73	MCW	Leyland
DMS 1452-1467	MLH452-467L	5/73-8/73	MCW	Gardner
DMS 1468-1499	MLH468-499L	6/73-9/73	MCW	Leyland
DMS 1500-1702	THM500-702M	8/73-9/74	MCW	Leyland
DM 1703-1720	THM703-720M	8/74-10/74	MCW	Leyland
DM 1721-1739	SMU721-739N	10/74	MCW	Leyland
DM 1740-1832	GHM740-832N	10/74-4/75	MCW	Leyland
DMS 1833-1897	GHM833-897N	3/75-8/75	MCW	Leyland
DMS 1898-1967	KUC898-967P	8/75-12/75	MCW	Leyland
DMS 1968	KUC968P	4/76	MCW	Rolls-Royce
DMS 1969-1999	KUC969-999P	4/76-7/76	MCW	Leyland
DMS 2000	KJD500P	6/76	MCW	Leyland
DMS 2001-2024	KJD1-24P	6/76-9/76	MCW	Leyland
DMS 2025-2037	OUC25-37R	9/76-10/76	MCW	Leyland
DMS 2038-2057	OUC38-57R	10/76-11/76	MCW	Gardner
DMS 2058	KJD58P	2/76	PRV	Leyland
DMS 2059	KJD59P	2/76	PRV	Rolls-Royce
DMS 2060-2119	KJD60-119P	2/76-6/76	PRV	Leyland
DMS 2120	KJD120P	6/76	PRV	Rolls-Royce
DMS 2121-2122	KJD121-122P	6/76	PRV	Leyland
DMS 2123-2127	OJD123-127R	8/76	PRV	Leyland
DMS 2128-2166	OJD128-166R	8/76-1/77	PRV	Gardner
DMS 2167-2246	OJD167-246R	11/76-6/77	MCW	Gardner
DMS 2247-2267	OJD247-267R	6/77-8/77	MCW	Leyland B20
DMS 2268-2346	THX268-346S	8/77-2/78	MCW	Leyland B20
DMS 2347-2472	OJD347-472R	1/77-8/77	PRV	Leyland B20
DMS 2473-2526	THX473-526S	8/77-12/77	PRV	Leyland B20
DM 2527-2646	THX527-646S	11/77-8/78	PRV	Leyland B20